Sacred Sites

of the world

Sacred Sites

of the world

Nirad Grover

Lustre Press
Roli Books

Contents

Following pages: *Aerial view of Bete Ghiorghis Church, Lalibela, Ethiopia.*

Confucius's Temple & Tomb
Qufu, China

It has been argued that Confucianism – a term coined by seventeenth-century Jesuit missionaries – is not a religion at all. Instead, it is an elucidation by its proponents, Confucius, followed by Mencius, Lao Tzu, and others, on the ethically correct way to live life. Certainly, it is true that this way does not revolve around concepts fundamental to the great religions of the world. Ideas such as the nature of God, of the soul, and of life after death are peripheral to Confucianism's main substance. This is due to the fact that Chinese religion developed in near-complete isolation from the rest of the world. Its steady emphasis was always on maintaining the balance in nature, and later, the Will of Heaven – a concept which became prevalent after the Shang period (1766-1122 BCE). This was understood as directed towards concern for the people, rather than obeisance to, and the fear of, an alternately benevolent and avenging God. It is the Will of Heaven then, the fountainhead of ethical values and their pursuance, that instates Confucianism into the realm of religion. It is expressly stated in one of the Four Books, ancient Chinese classics of Confucianism, that the sage, upon gaining true integrity, is united with Heaven and Earth.

Confucius, the greatest of the great sages, was born to a humble family in 551 BCE. Working his way through modest jobs, he acquired the requisite merit to be appointed as Minister of Justice in his home

Facing page: Image of Confucius, at the temple of Qufu, his birthplace.

The Sage's statue stands tall over a public gathering.

state of Lu. Some years later, he resigned from the post and travelled through the region, disseminating his wisdom. The essence of the wisdom is summed up in his Golden Rule, 'Do not do to others what you would not want others to do to you.' According to him, the desired goal of an ideal society was possible only by imbibing virtuous personal qualities. These included humaneness, a sense of justice, placing the interests of others before oneself, respect to elders, and reverence for ancestors. Rituals and rules of etiquette were prescribed for such conduct. Steadfast adherence to these would ultimately lead to sagehood.

Confucius died at the age of seventy-three in his hometown,

Qufu. Two years later, the Sacred First Teacher's house was declared a temple. Over the centuries, it suffered several depredations by fire, only to be rebuilt each time on a grander scale. By the end of the fifteenth century the scale of the complex stood second only to Beijing's Imperial Palace. Today, it has a more than a hundred buildings and 460 rooms. The rectangular sprawl, extending along an axis of nine courtyards and preliminary gates, climaxes at the Dacheng Hall (Hall of Great Perfection). Built during the Qing period, it is the primary place for ceremonies, and one of the finest examples of traditional Chinese architecture. Ten rock pillars, carved with coiled dragons, support its front. Facing it, recalling Confucius's' lectures to his disciples delivered under an apricot tree, is the Apricot Platform, whereas the hall behind is dedicated to his wife. The sage's own home is, however, gone. The temple is a showcase of Chinese art spanning more than 2000 years and several dynasties. The main buildings are elegant structures with yellow-tiled upward-curving roofs. Amongst the hundreds of stelae are the pavilions of Jin, Yuan, Song and Qing dynasties.

Confucius was buried north of Qufu on the banks of the Si river. Soon after his passing, the axe-shaped (now cone-shaped) tomb became a place of pilgrimage. Just as the area around his home was transformed into a temple, over the centuries, the precincts of his burial place grew into a family cemetery of staggering scale. More than 100,000 of his descendants, spanning nearly eighty generations, lie beneath the grass and cypress covered grounds. They are remembered with tombstones, sculptures, pillars and gates, venerated at dozens of stelae pavilions and sacrificial halls, and segregated from the rest of the world by a seven-kilometre perimeter wall.

Living generations of Confucius's' lineage were housed in the nearby Kong family mansion. Swelling to no less than 150 buildings and three times as many rooms, the housing complex kept up with its complementary compounds. All its components were located to conform to the principles of orderly society

preached by the original head of the family. Thus, the official buildings are in front, the residential quarters behind them, and the gardens right at the back. Duke Yan Sheng, as the senior direct descendant was hereditarily titled, lived in the central residential building. East of this, in the Yi Gun Hall, dwelt his younger brother. Servants and masters were appropriately compartmentalised, and so were men and women. Together, the entire workforce kept alive the legacy of the Great Master. They nurtured the vast temple, and tended the cemetery, doing for their ancestors as they would have their descendants do for them.

Gate of the Great Bear, one of the series of portals leading up to the Hall of Great Perfection.

St Mark's Cathedral
Cairo, Egypt

St Mark the Evangelist, one of Jesus Christ's twelve apostles, walked into Alexandria in the middle of the first century with a torn sandal. He found a cobbler, Anianus, and asked him to fix his ragged footwear. Anianus, while working on it, accidentally pierced his finger with the needle. St Mark smeared his hand with mud, wet it with his spit, and applied it on Anianus's hand. The hand healed immediately, and Anianus and his family were evangelized. Though Christianity had already trickled into Egypt before he arrived, it is St Mark who is recognized as the official founder of the religion in Egypt, and all of Africa. Later, a church was built over the site of the shoemaker's home. This was the first building of the Cathedral of St Mark, and that of the Coptic Orthodox Church in the world.

The Copts emerged as a distinct community at the Council of Chalcedon, called by Roman Emperor Marcianus in c. CE 450 to resolve simmering differences within Christianity. However, the Council failed to reconcile what proved to be the major contentious issue, a disagreement pertaining to the nature of Christ. While one side asserted his dual nature – human as well as divine – the other maintained that Christ exists in one nature alone, in which both the human and divine coexist. The Council ratified the 'dual' belief, and those who opposed it, departed to be known as the Oriental Orthodox Church. The Coptic Orthodox Church is

Facing page: *The Coptic Cross is recognizable with its broad arms, each with three points.*

A monk burns incense at a Coptic ceremony. Today, both Arabic and Coptic are employed for Church services in Egypt.

regarded as the spiritual umbrella of this community.

The final incarnation of the Egyptian language, Coptic is a construction of the Greek alphabet supplemented with a sprinkling of the Demotic script. Coptic emerged in the second century and was spoken well into the seventeenth century, when it finally succumbed to Arabic. It exists today as a language of the Coptic Church, much in the same way that Latin is the language of the Roman Catholic Church. The head of the Coptic Orthodox Church is known as the Pope of Alexandria and Patriarch of All Africa on the Holy See of St Mark. Alexandria's cathedral, along with some other churches in Egypt, is his seat.

The present church building is not old. Comprehensive phases of rebuilding took place in the nineteenth century, and in the early 1950s, it was completely reconstructed. Further renewals took place in the late 1980s. However, episodes in the church's history go back two thousand years. The first major event was St Mark's death. Threatened by the new religion he preached, the pagan Egyptians captured him and dragged him through the streets of Alexandria. After he died, they tried to burn his body but the Christians retrieved it and buried it in the church. In the ninth century, the relics were stolen by Venetian merchant-sailors and housed in a basilica built in Venice dedicated to the Saint. However, Coptic belief says that the head did not leave Alexandria. Meanwhile, the church had already been ruined and rebuilt once, after the Arab conquest of Egypt in the seventh century. It took another beating during the time of the Crusades, and was knocked down yet again during the French invasion of Alexandria, in the closing years of the eighteenth century.

Coptic art is a distinct style which evolved out of the mix of Egyptian and Hellenistic influences in the early Christian period. Its human iconography is distinguishable by large eyes and small mouths. The Cathedral's new mosaics include icons of the Saints Mary, George, Mina, Anthony and Mark. The latter is often depicted with his symbol, the lion, which stems from his likening of John the Baptist to the regal beast of the desert. Another story tells of the power of his prayer, through which he eliminated two lions that threatened his father and himself as they travelled through Jordan. The broad lines of the Coptic cross, displayed prominently in the church, have three-pointed ends. While each threesome stands for the Father, Son and the Holy Spirit, together they represent the twelve apostles of Christ.

The months of the Coptic calendar derive their names from ancient Egyptian deities or feasts. In the month of Babah (October-November), which traces its origins to an annual feast at the famous temple of Luxor, the Coptics celebrate the church's consecration and sighting of its founder's head in Alexandria. The rest of the Evangelist's remains continue to lie in Venice – except for a bone relic that was returned in 1968 by the Roman Catholic pope. It is now the cherished possession of the humble home that became a modern church.

Pope Shenouda III, current head of the Coptic Orthodox Church.

Church of the Nativity
Bethlehem, Israel

One winter night, in the closing years of the first century BCE, a small group of men followed the path shown by a star over the Mediterranean kingdom of Judea. The star led them to a manger in the town of Bethlehem. They had been told that here, in this modest place, the king of Jews had been born, and they carried him gifts. The men came to be known as the Magi, and the newborn was Jesus, son of Mary and the Holy Spirit. So goes the story of Nativity, told by the Gospels of Luke and Matthew, in the New Testament of the Bible. It is one of the best-known stories in the world, the protagonist probably the most influential man of all time, and the day of his birth the most widely celebrated single event

across the world. Christianity today embraces one-third of humanity.

Three hundred years after Jesus Christ ('Christ' means the Messiah) had lived out his short but intense life, his following had increased exponentially. Christianity was now an organized religion, with a growing corpus of literature and number of, usually persecuted, adherents. A big turn in their fortunes came when Constantine, previously a pantheist, became the first Roman Emperor to convert to Christianity. Bethlehem was then a part of the ascendant Byzantine Empire, and it received the attentions of Constantine's mother, Helena. The first basilica over Jesus' birthplace was raised by her, only to be totally destroyed in the sixth century, during the revolt of

Facing page: *Bell tower, Church of the Nativity – one of the oldest standing Christian structures in the world.*

A nun kisses the spot where Jesus Christ was born.

the Samaritans. Emperor Justinian responded in the second half of the same century by rebuilding it as an even larger structure. From then on it stayed erect, despite the turmoil that was to rage around it for times to come. Fifty years after Justinian, the Persians attacked Bethlehem, laying the city waste but sparing the basilica, apparently because their general noticed that the three Magi, as shown in a mosaic inside, were in Persian garb. Down the centuries, Jesus's original home was defended fiercely by the Crusaders and Muslims alike, an experience testified to by its fortress-like demeanour. The latest test came in 2002 when Israeli forces besieged the basilica in pursuit of

Palestinian fighters who had taken shelter within its hallowed interior. At least ten people were killed in the ensuing skirmish though the building remained intact. Today it stands as the oldest functioning Church in the world.

The focus of reverence is inside a dimly-lit 36-square-metre grotto situated below the sanctuary. Two sets of stairs, converging at the bottom, lead down to it. The walls of the almost rectangular chamber are clad in marble and decorated with a tapestry depicting events from Jesus's childhood. An altar is placed over what is believed to be the exact site of Jesus's birth. Embedded on the sacred spot is a fourteen-pointed star, inscribed on which are the Latin words De Virgine Maria Jesus Christus Natus Est – 1717. They tell the story simply: 'Here Jesus Christ was born to the Virgin Mary'; the date refers to when the inscription was inserted by the Catholic clergy. The fifteen silver lamps hanging around it are related to the Greek Orthodox, Latin and Armenian Christian communities historically associated with the church. There are two more altars: one marks the manger where the infant Jesus was set down after his arrival into the world, and the other is dedicated to the Magi. Several other items like ornaments, figurines of saints, and more hanging lamps and lamp stands add to the décor of the underground cavity.

Outside, the main sanctuary is shielded by an intricately-carved wooden iconostasis. Beyond it stretches the nave. The stone-slab floor was laid by the Greeks in the nineteenth century, and the pointed ceiling consists of cedar wood rafters dating back to the fourteenth century. The rounded arms of the two transepts stretch out into the compound where the Greek Orthodox, Armenian and Roman Catholic convents are located. The nave is simple yet impressive, chiefly because of the forty-four six-metre-tall Corinthian columns arranged in four rows. Originally, the columns had beautiful frescoes which have all but disappeared. The walls too were once a feast of mosaic art. Now most of what remains is on the lower level – one rendition is identifiable as figures of Jesus's ancestors.

Clerestory windows allow bright light on to the nave. However, the vestibule is dark and gloomy. The door at the nave end bears panels created by Armenian craftsmen in the thirteenth century. As for the main entrance door, it was designed by the Ottomans to prevent horsemen from riding into the Church. Considerably less than one-and-a-half metres high, it requires even a walking visitor to bend down. The Door of Humility, as it is named, reminds one that small beginnings can eventually end up larger than life.

Christmas trees, lights and fireworks light up the Church of the Nativity during New Year's Eve celebrations for the new millennium.

Mural depicting the Nativity, which is the name given to the account of Jesus Christ's birth, in a manger in Bethlehem.

Bodhgaya
India

Ensconced for years in a life of luxury, young Prince Siddhartha Gautama, once exposed to the general populace, was bewildered by and unable to accept the sickness, pain and unhappiness he saw. Finally, driven by a desire to find a reason and solution for the suffering, he renounced his family and royal life, and roamed the country as a beggar, subjecting himself to extreme deprivation. However, he discovered that this way of life also led to sickness and misery. So he sat down under a banyan tree at Bodhgaya and continued his quest through meditation. After forty-nine days, Siddhartha attained nirvana or Enlightenment. Henceforth he was known as the Buddha or the 'Awakened One'.

The Buddha taught the Four Noble Truths, which explained the causes of suffering were ignorance and attachment, and that the way to overcome them was through the Eightfold Path. This comprised right mindfulness, right concentration, right understanding, right thought, right speech, right effort, right action, and right livelihood. His teachings inspired the birth of one of the greatest religions of the world – Buddhism.

The Buddha lived in the sixth century BCE. Four sites associated with his life are considered most holy for Buddhists: his birthplace at Lumbini, in Nepal; Bodhgaya; Sarnath, where he gave his first sermon; and Kushinagar, where he took leave of his body. Of these, Bodhgaya occupies the highest

Facing page: *The Buddha's footprints carved in stone at the Mahabodhi Temple in Bodhgaya.*

24

eminence. Before leaving for Sarnath, he is said to have visited seven different places here, over a period of seven weeks. These are now in the precincts of the Mahabodhi Mahavihara or Great Temple Complex.

The first week was spent under the Bodhi Tree, the place of his Enlightenment. In the third century BCE, the Mauryan Emperor Ashoka, ruler of India's first great empire, converted to Buddhism. His children carried a sapling of the Bodhi Tree to Anuradhapura in Sri Lanka. When the Bodhgaya tree died, a sapling was brought back from Anuradhapura and planted in its place. Underneath this tree is a stone slab where the Buddha is said to have attained nirvana. The second week was spent at the Animeshlochana Stupa, from where he stared unblinkingly at the Bodhi Tree. The location is now marked by a small white temple. Carved stone lotuses indicate points on the raised platform of the Jewel Walk or the Ratnachankrama where he spent the third week walking and meditating. In the fourth week, he meditated on the highest laws behind existence, at a place now marked by the Ratnagraha Chaitya or temple. As he did so, his body is believed to have emanated blue, yellow, red, white and orange hues. These are now the colours of the Buddhist flag.

Sitting under the Ajapala Nigrodha Tree, the Buddha spent the fifth week in discussion with a Brahmin (Hindu priest), explaining that it is one's deeds and not one's birth that define a man. In the penultimate week, he meditated again. This time it was beside the Muchhalinda or Lotus Pond, abode of the Serpent King, who gave him protection. There is a life-like depiction of this scene in the middle of the pond. And finally, during the last seven days, the Buddha is said to have sat under the Rajyatana Tree, of which the exact location is not known but a spot has nevertheless been identified for worship.

The present fifty-metre-high Mahabodhi Mahavihara is built on top of a temple constructed by Ashoka; part of the temple railings are from that period. An ornate *torana* or gateway leads to the inner courtyard where a large stone with the Buddha's footprints is enshrined. His gilded statue in the *bhumisparsha mudra*, that is, with one finger pointing towards the earth, is in the inner sanctum.

Devotees at Bodhgaya prostrate themselves, and rotate their personal prayer wheels, each turn of which is meant to absolve them of sins accrued. Butter lamps shed a golden glow on the temple, and soft murmurs of prayers and chanting float through the incense filled air, broken only by occasional gongs from the many monasteries established in the area.

Lighting candles at the stupas inside the complex.

25

Kaaba

Mecca, Saudi Arabia

It was during the time of Adam and Eve that the Black Stone plummeted down from the sky. It was sent down by God to signify the link between Heaven and Earth. At that point in time, the Stone shone pure and white. But over the centuries, it soaked in the sins of humans and turned black. Around 2000 BCE, Abraham, the first great prophet, built a cuboid house, or kaaba (in Arabic), over the holy relic. So believe the Muslims.

At the time of Muhammad's birth in c. 570 BCE, the burning sands of Arabia were the home of warring tribes, worshipping pagan gods. Muhammad, belonging to the tribe of Quraysh, was happily married and lived the prosperous life of a trader. At the age of forty, he began experiencing visions and revelations from above. The main message was that there is but one God, Allah, and all others are false. Life began to get difficult for Muhammad in Mecca, his hometown, when he began preaching this message. Considered a disruptor, he was compelled to leave his hometown with a small band of followers. The group settled in Medina, 340 kilometres north of Mecca, where the Prophet's ideas were received more favourably. The number of Muslims (literally 'those

Facing page: *Pilgrims at the Kaaba on Laylet al-Qadr (Night of Power), one of Islam's holiest nights, when the Quran began to be revealed to the Prophet Muhammad.*

Muslims express reverence at the sacred Black Stone, ensconced in the eastern corner of the Kaaba.

who submit to God') increased, and through battle, diplomacy and political manoeuvring, they grew strong enough to eventually subjugate Mecca.

It is a fact that both the Stone and the Kaaba existed before the birth of Muhammad, the founder of Islam. This was one place where people of all denominations congregated and brushed shoulders in peace, as it also housed the numerous deities of the region, including some Egyptian, Christian and Jewish images. After taking the city in 630 CE, one of Muhammad's first tasks was to clear the Kaaba and its environs of all idols and make it a place of Muslim worship only. From that day, it has remained the spiritual centre of Islam – the

second largest religion in the world.

Though the sway of Islamic power over Mecca has never been broken, the Kaaba has been subject to demolition, rebuilding and repair. The present structure is made in black granite mined in the nearby hills, and rises about thirteen metres above the ground. Its sides measure approximately twelve metres each. The corners are oriented towards the four compass points. A black cloth, called the *kiswah*, embroidered with Quranic verses in gold, drapes the sacred cuboid. A portal in the north-eastern wall is the only entrance. Set two metres above ground level, it is accessible by a wheeled wooden staircase, usually stored elsewhere. Inside, there are more inscriptions from the Quran (Muslim holy book) on a green cloth, as well as on the walls it partly covers.

Muslims hold that the gate to Heaven lies over the Kaaba, and the seat of Allah is in the seventh Heaven above it. When Muhammad rededicated the shrine to Allah, he circumambulated it seven times. This ritual encircling, called Tawaf, accompanied with recitation of verses from the Quran, continues to be an essential part of the worship. The irregularly-shaped Black Stone is placed on the eastern corner. Broken, and even stolen once, during the rough and tumble of medieval history, it was put back together, and is now framed in silver. Though the circling pilgrims seek to touch or kiss it, the prevailing hustle and bustle renders that an unlikely privilege. In compromise, they point to it on each pass.

Islamic tradition says that the city of Mecca owes its origin to the well called Zamzam. The story goes that, left in the desert with her baby Ishmael, Hagar, Abraham's wife, was running out of food and water. Desperate, she deposited the infant on the ground, and sought the vantage points of two neighbouring hills to look out for help. As her son was out of sight when she traversed the valley in between, she ran to cover this distance fast. She did this seven times before God interceded and a spring erupted where Ishmael lay. The two hills, Safah and Marwah, fall within the boundaries of the Al-Haram Mosque, which encloses the Kaaba. Hagar's efforts are

emulated by pilgrims, who walk through a marked corridor between the two acclivities. Water from the well, formed by the spring, is revered.

In the twelfth month of the Muslim calendar, the massive Al-Haram Mosque is flooded by an ocean of pious humanity. This is the time of the Hajj, or annual pilgrimage to Mecca, which is one of the 'Five Pillars' (duties) of Islam. Unless shackled by health or financial reasons, every Muslim is obliged to make the journey at least once in their lifetime. Muhammad the Prophet's first Hajj was his triumphant return to the city of his birth. It was also his last. He went back to Medina and died there two years later.

A painting of the Kaaba and the annual Hajj via modern modes of transport, on a Mecca wall.

St Peter's Basilica
Vatican City

By the third century, the Roman Empire had grown too big for its own good. Emperor Diocletian, aiming to make his cumbersome and restless dominions more manageable, divided the Empire into Eastern and Western parts. The East was governed from Constantinople and the West from Ravenna, and then Milan. No longer the political focus of the Mediterranean and the conquered European world, the splendid city of Rome went into decline. However, before the Western Empire fell apart, two developments ensured that through its dark years, Rome's light would diminish but not extinguish. One was the establishment of the papacy. The second was the Basilica erected by Emperor Constantine, that great saviour of the Christians, over St Peter's grave. Together, they would provide the force and the platform which, when the time again became ripe, would explode as the glorious centre of a rejuvenated Rome.

Peter, considered first amongst Christ's twelve apostles, was crucified and buried in Rome in 61 CE. He was the founder of Christianity in Rome. The Pope is recognized as his successor, as well as the Vicar of Christ and the worldwide spiritual head of the Roman Catholic Church. As Rome struggled through its difficult years, the papacy floundered but held itself together. By the eighth century, the legacy of the Western Roman Empire had been appropriated by a federation of central European states going by

Facing page: *Detail from the mosaic* Apparition of the Heart of Jesus to St Mary Margaret, *decorating the Altar of the Sacred Heart in St Peter's Basilica. The altar is one of about twenty-five in the Basilica.*

Michelangelo's dome forms the roof over Bernini's baldacchino, which shelters the papal altar and St Peter's relics.

More than 1100 years into its first incarnation by now, St Peter's Basilica was not in the best of shape. Pope Nicholas V decided to something about it. From the time he began the demolition of the old building in 1452 to the consecration of the new building in 1626, eighteen popes blessed and witnessed the project. More importantly, virtually the who's who of the Renaissance's creative line-up, as well as many Mannerist and Baroque virtuosos, contributed to it. The result was awesome.

The first impression of the Basilica – since 1929, a part of the independent Vatican state, within Rome – is of the enormity of its scale. The arrow-straight road from the teeming city breaks into a massive piazza enclosed with semi-circular Doric colonnades designed by the Baroque architect Giovanni Bernini. From the centre of the enormous space rises an Egyptian obelisk, first brought to Rome by Emperor Caligula in the first century, and raised here in the sixteenth century in complete silence, as a symbol of Christianity's

the nomenclature of the Holy Roman Empire. Unified by Latin Christianity, the Empire beheld the Pope as its spiritual head. Nevertheless, despite being protected by the Holy Roman Emperors, the papacy remained insecure. By the fifteenth century, however, it had recharged and consolidated its resources. The Church was now plump with wealth, and its custodians, the popes, were itching to reassert their religion's and their own dominance. The Renaissance had begun in Italy. Rome's time had come again.

victory over pagan faiths. The cross at its pinnacle is said to contain the relics of Christ's True Cross. The fifty-metre-high palatial façade of the Basilica is propped up by Corinthian columns. Again in Baroque style, Carlo Maderno's design is perfect for the Pope to stand at the balcony and bless the thronging crowds below. Past the main entrance into the Basilica is the Porta Santa, or the Holy Door, which is traditionally kept walled up and opened personally by the Pope for the course of a designated Holy Year. A window in the apse lights up an image of the Holy Spirit as a dove. Dominating the nave is Bernini's ornamental baldacchino of gilded bronze. It covers the main altar at which only the Pope can celebrate Mass. Underneath it is St Peter's subterranean crypt, from which two-and-a-half hectares of magnificence radiates.

Some way off from the Basilica, on Janiculum hillside, is the site of St. Peter's crucifixion. In the early sixteenth century, Donato Bramante designed the Tempietto San Pietro here. Displaying all the elements of classical antiquity, the Tempietto is considered Rome's first true Renaissance building. Its drum, dome and Doric columns served as the prototypal essence of the Basilica's central plan, for which Bramante was commissioned by Pope Julius II. He was succeeded by another Renaissance giant, Raphael, much of whose handiwork was later altered. However, the creative instinct behind the Basilica's masterpiece, its dome, was Michelangelo's.

At the age of seventy-one, Michelangelo was persuaded to

The Basilica's front façade, as seen from St Peter's Square. At the base of the obelisk in the centre of the Square are four couchant lions, each with two bodies and intertwining tails.

33

Pope Benedict XVI (elected 2005) prostrates himself on the ground before the altar during a Good Friday ceremony inside the Basilica.

Following pages: St Peter's at dusk. In the foreground is the ancient St. Angelo bridge, spanning the Tiber river.

take over as chief architect of St Peter's. His conditions: he would work "for the love of the Saint", without payment, without interference, and without accounting responsibilities. He probably got the deal he wanted, though his hemispherical design was changed to an ovoid shape due to structural concerns. Almost 140 metres high, the dome gets its skeletal strength from sixteen externally visible radial ribs. One can climb up to the base of the lantern for a sweeping view of the symmetrical piazza. The inner shell looms over the baldacchino. Embellished with scores of frescoes, its curvature soars up to a bright climax. Medallions of saints are ranged around the base. Around it, in letters two metres high, are words from the Gospel of Matthew. They recall of the true reason for the sumptuous art and grandeur all around: "Thou art Peter, and upon this rock I will build my Church ... I will give you the keys to the Kingdom of Heaven ..." The Keys are below, carved on the base of the altar canopy, as part of Pope Urban VIII's coat of arms.

Temple Mount
Jerusalem, Israel

The last bit of uneven rock that protrudes from the top of Mount Moriah is the holiest spot in Judaism. Jews identify it as the foundation stone of the world laid by God. On it, at God's behest, Abraham almost sacrificed his son Isaac, and Jacob, son of Isaac, dreamt of the ladder to Heaven used by the angels. In the tenth century BCE, King Solomon erected the First Jewish Temple on top of the rise – hence the name Temple Mount – at the centre of which was the Rock. On this stone was installed the Ark of the Covenant, in which were kept the tablets inscribed with the Ten Commandments revealed to Moses by God. A chamber, called the Holy of Holies, was built over this. Only the High Priest was allowed to enter it.

The Temple was rebuilt following its destruction by the Babylonians in the sixth century BCE, and expanded by Herod the Great in the first century, around the time Christianity was born. Jesus is supposed to have prayed on the Rock, and in the fourth century, Helena, mother of the first Christian Roman Emperor, Constantine, raised a church on the hill. Comparatively, Christendom's attachment to the Mount is least amongst the three religions. And even though Islam was born six hundred years after Christianity, the Mount holds much more spiritual and physical significance for it. After Mecca and Medina, it is Islam's third-most revered site.

During his early days in Medina, in acknowledgement of the prophetic primacy of Abraham, Muhammad

Facing page: *Inscriptions of verses from the Quran run around the octagonal-drum base of the Dome of the Rock shrine on the Temple Mount.*

Turkish tiles, copies of the sixteenth-century tiles added by Suleiman the Magnificent, adorn the Domes exteriors.

positioned his qibla (direction of prayer) towards Jerusalem. Additionally, the Quran relates the story of the Prophet's fateful night journey to Heaven, summoned by God, with the archangel Gabriel as escort. The first part of the journey, the Isra, began from the 'the most sacred mosque', the Kaaba. Woken from his sleep, Muhammad was whisked away on the winged horse Buraq to 'the farthest mosque', believed by Muslims to be at the Rock on the Temple Mount. On the second phase of his divine excursion, called Mi'raj, he was transported to Heaven, where he met earlier prophets like Moses and Abraham, and was given an audience by God himself.

A few years after the Prophet's death, Umar, the second Caliph, captured Jerusalem. He cleared the rubbish dump that the Mount area had been reduced to by the Romans, paid his respects at the Rock, and ordered that a mosque be built at some distance from it, in the direction of Mecca. The intention was to clearly emphasise to Muslims the precedence of the Kaaba over the Rock, which is foremost to the Judaic religion. However, some years later, the Umayyad Caliph Abd al-Malik visited Jerusalem, and giving the Rock its own due, commissioned a dome over it. The motivation could also have been to exceed existing Christian churches in magnificence. While the original wooden Al-Aqsa ('farthest') Mosque was rebuilt over the centuries, the Dome of the Rock, apart from renovations, has survived

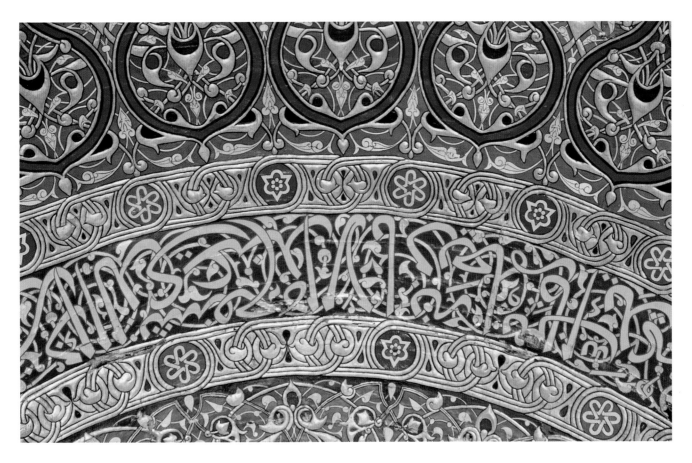

in its original form. Today, not only is it the oldest surviving Muslim monument, but is also recognized as one of the finest examples of Muslim religious architecture.

The last major rebuilding of Al-Aqsa was in the eleventh century. It has seven bays, of which the three main ones are in Romanesque style. There are several pillars and halls inside, and much of the decoration, including the ceiling, dates from the twentieth century. In contrast to the Mosque's lead-sheeted dome, the Dome of the Rock gleams with gold leaf. Both the drum on which it stands and the closed arcade around it, are octagonal. The stunning tile-work on the façade was originally the handiwork of sixteenth-century craftsmen, sponsored by the

Ottoman Sultan, Suleiman the Magnificent. Two rows of inscriptions running around the base of the dome and the octagonal exterior walls below relate the story of Muhammad's nocturnal sojourn to Allah's abode, and speak of His glory. The interior calligraphy records the contribution of various rulers to the building's embellishment, and also articulates through Quranic verses that Jesus was a Prophet, and not the son of God as claimed by Christians. Rich mosaics and carvings in floral and geometric patterns decorate the surfaces of the ceiling and the two concentric arched galleries. Ensconced behind a wooden screen is the Rock. Under it is a cavity, in which, it is said, that the dead meet to pray and await the Day of Judgement.

Floral patterns and calligraphy inside the shrine.

With the sun shining on it, the Dome of the Rock is Jerusalem's most recognisable landmark.

If there is one site where the three Abrahamic religions superimpose inextricably upon one another, it is the Temple Mount. Though all three faiths have the same roots, they have branched differently, and perhaps because of their common lineage, have found all the more need to assert themselves unequivocally and uncompromisingly against one another. Their relationship has always been uneasy and volatile, and Jerusalem, the legendary city of the Holy Bible and the Quran has borne much of the fallout.

Though Israeli forces captured Jerusalem from the Arabs in 1967, they considered it prudent for the sake of peace to let status quo remain on the Mount. Thus, while Muslims continue to control the hill, the Christian focus in Jerusalem is on another small hill called Golgotha, the place of Jesus's crucifixion. The Jews, denied their ruined Temple, lament its destruction at a section of the Mount's outer wall known as the Western Wall – the last major surviving feature of Herod's great building around the original location of the Ark.

Holy City of Touba
Senegal

Sufism, the mystical form of Islam, was born in the eighth century in Iraq. Its essential doctrine lays down that the way to reach the Divine, who exists in and as everything, is through personal communion. To do this, one must shed all conceptions of the individual self and devote one's whole being, through prayer, meditation and the guidance of an enlightened teacher, to realization of the formless 'Ultimate Truth'. Over the years, Sufism branched out into many tariqas, or orders. Almost all claim that their way and beliefs originate from the Prophet himself, and were transmitted down by his cousin and son-in-law Ali, and disciple Uwais. Sufism soon spread all over the Muslim world, reaching Senegal

relatively late, at the end of the medieval period.

There are four Sufi orders in Senegal. Of these, the Mouride is the second largest and the most influential. Its founder, Ahmadou Bamba, was himself born to a mahabout, or spiritual leader of another larger order, the Qaidiriya, in 1853. Bamba developed his own philosophy, of which there were two major facets. One was pacifism, which manifested in his dogged but peaceful opposition to French colonial rule in Senegal. The French exiled him, but later realized that this only led to an increase in his following, and that his message did not, in any case, encourage violent unrest. They allowed him to return. Bamba's other emphasis was on the ethic of hard work. This

Facing page: The Great Mosque of Touba, considered one of the largest in Africa, was completed in 1963. The central minaret, named Lamp Fall, is one of the country's most well-known edifices.

Interiors of Touba's Great Mosque

is the reason why the Mourides are comparatively an economically well-off group.

Touba existed only as the nondescript shadow of a tree on the remote Senegalese landscape where Bamba is said to have had a transcendental experience of the divine. It became Bamba's place of propagation and, in 1927, the site of his burial. The settlement rapidly grew into the centre of Mouridism and the entire city is considered holy by the sect's adherents. The city's special status bestows all administrative power over it to the Mouride community, who ensure that the sacredness of the place is maintained through a ban on liquor, tobacco and certain unacceptable social activities. One of Bamba's most revered disciples was Ibrahim Fall, an uneducated but charismatic man who made up for his lack of intellectual ability by immersing himself in physical labour, as per his leader's call. Ibrahim gained his own sub-following. Called Baye Fall, its members are distinctly identifiable by hair worn as matted locks, torn and unkempt apparel, and unabashed soliciting for donations. Every year Touba is inundated with hundreds of thousands of devotees converging on the city as part of the Grand Magal pilgrimage. During this time, the somewhat

Mouride followers wait at the Great Mosque's doors at the time of the Grand Magal pilgrimage

intimidating Baye Fall assume a policing role, carrying clubs and keeping an eye on the milling crowds.

Ibrahim Fall's memory is kept aloft by a grand minaret that soars highest amongst the five that rise from Touba's Great Mosque. Begun by Bamba himself, the enormous Mosque is topped by three big domes and clusters of small blister-like blue eruptions. At the apex of the Mouride religious hierarchy is the Grand Marabout. Amadou Bamba was the first, and the line of leadership is hereditary. His five sons who succeeded to the title are buried near the Mosque.

Islam holds Muhammad to be the last of the Prophets. However, Bamba's followers claim that according to the Hadith tradition, which expounds on Muhammad's words and actions, 'renewers of the faith' are sent by Allah every hundred years. They believe their original leader to be one such renewer. In Touba, images of Bamba are everywhere – his pictures are on private and public transport, they hang in homes and offices, and are painted on walls and displayed in shops. Most derive from a black and white picture, in which the Grand Marabout stands outside his home with his face covered. Taken in the early 1900s, it is the only known photograph of the first Mouride.

48

Gomateshwara Statue
Sravanabelagola, India

The sixth century BCE was a period of disenchantment with the prevailing Vedic religion in India. Tightly controlled by the priestly class, it had become a complex construct of rituals and restrictions, which did not alleviate the fundamental problem of life: sorrow. There was a desire to find a simpler and economically less burdensome way to mitigate misery and achieve spiritual contentment. Jainism was born in this milieu. Jain tradition holds that there have been twenty-four tirthankaras (ford-makers) or saints, of which Vardhamana was the last. Born in a royal family, the prince became an ascetic, and after years of meditation arrived upon the true way to live life and attain salvation. He was thereafter known as Jina, or

'Conqueror', and Mahavira, or 'Great Hero'. By the first century CE, Jainsim had established itself in eastern and western India, and by the fourth century, it was truly an all-India religion.

Jainism believes in an eternal universe, rather than in an eternal god. Everything in the universe has a soul and interacts with each other in consonance with natural law. Moksha or salvation from the cycle of birth and rebirth can only be achieved through the right personal conduct. Principal to this is the practice of non-violence, respect for all forms of life, truthfulness, celibacy, and ultimately, detachment. In the second century, the faith split into two sects, the Digambara or sky-clad and the Shwetambara or

Facing page: *Devotional offering runs down Gomateshwara's handsome visage. The statue is a fine example of medieval art produced by the Western Ganga dynasty.*

white-clad. The differences were minor, and not doctrinal.

Of uncertain antiquity, Adinatha was the first tirthankara in the tradition of great Jain teachers. The legend goes that, upon his abdication, his two sons, Bharata and Bahubali, clashed with each other over the throne. Bahubali, the more spiritual one, was troubled by his conscience over fighting with his brother, and renounced the kingdom and all material life. He became an ascetic, immersed himself in meditation, and came to be revered as Gomateshwara, the 'Handsome One'. In the tenth century, a part of southern India was ruled by the Western Ganga dynasty, under which Jainism was a favoured religion. Chamundaraya, an influential military commander of the regime, was of a literary and religious bent. He commissioned a massive statue of Gomateshwara on top of Vindhyagiri hill, at Sravanabelagola.

The statue is carved out of a single block of granite and soars eighteen metres above the hill. For Digambaras, abnegating material possessions also includes the shedding of clothes. As such, Gomateshwara is portrayed standing serenely naked. Vines hewn creeping up his thighs convey the

enduring immobility maintained by him in deep contemplation. Over 600 steps lead from the base of the hill to the toes of the monolith. The gigantic figure can be seen from twenty-five kilometres away.

Once every twelve years, more than half of the world's Jain population converges at the statue for the Mahamastakabhisheka, an eleven-day festival replete with ceremonies. Carrying urns filled with water or coconut water, chanting worshippers slowly make their way upto the summit of the stone immensity via a scaffolding erected specially for the purpose. Once there, they pour the contents onto the statue in an act of devotion. The final anointing is done by priests from huge vessels containing more of the same liquids, as well as yoghurt, clarified butter, sugarcane juice, sandalwood oil, milk, saffron, precious stones and vermillion. The din of drums and applause accompanies the proceedings as the crowds below are drenched with the holy wash raining from above. The curtain is brought down with a showering of flowers. These are picked up by devotees from where they drop at the feet of Gomateshwara. They are believed to bring luck and protection.

Above: *Devotees surrender themselves to the climactic drenching on the Mahamastakabhisheka festival.*

Facing page: *Bahubali's monolith is one of the world's tallest free standing statues. It is said that the prince meditated in the erect yogic position for one year.*

At the feet of the monolith.

Lalibela Churches
Ethiopia

In the seventh century, after more than 1000 years of paramountcy over Ethiopia, the Aksumite kingdom was on the wane. Unable to withstand the insatiable Islamic armies pouring out from Arabia, Ethiopia's Oriental Orthodox Christians retreated into the natural sanctuary of the central uplands. This rugged land of volcanic rock was the perfect place to lie low and nurture their faith. The most enduring legacy of this period of closeted religious pursuit was to be later recognised as one of the finest examples of rock-cut architecture anywhere in the world, ever.

Gebrel Mesquel, the man who would be king of Ethiopia, was born to the Zagwe royal line in the mid twelfth century. It is said that his mother interpreted the swarm of bees buzzing over the newborn as an omen of his great destiny. He was thus called Lalibela, or one 'who the bees recognise as the sovereign'. Lalibela survived the determined attempts of his insecure relatives to kill him before he could fulfill his mother's prophecy, and ascended the throne. Two years before his crowning, the Muslims had taken Jerusalem. Lalibela had travelled to the Holy Land, and devout Christian that he was, was aware of the Biblical construct of New Jerusalem – a figurative, completely new Jerusalem, where all the saints would eventually live together. He reckoned it was time to build the divine city.

Sponsored and spurred by him, masons, sculptors and artisans set about chiselling and cutting into

Facing page: A prayer session in the dark depths of a Lalibela church is lit up for a few minutes by a beam of light streaming in.

Sunlight finds its way onto a church floor through a cross-shaped opening in the roof.

the rock of Roha, the town which later came to be called Lalibela. Approximately 2500 metres above sea level and guarded by the peak of Abuna Joseph, Lalibela's dream took shape. Complemented by a bewildering maze of narrow, interconnecting passages and galleries, about eleven churches were chipped and hammered out of the living rock. Hidden below the horizon, some were excavated at subterranean levels. Others were carved in open quarries. The word Roha is thought to have derived from the Arabic 'rawaha', which means 'a low plain of abundant water'. Indeed, the site has natural water wells lying deep in the earth, and these were tapped in a

feat of ingenious engineering. Additionally, a channel called the Yourdannus or Jordan river was grooved out between the edifices.

The churches are mainly grouped into northern and eastern complexes. Though the size and plan of each is different, some features are common to a few. Bete Medhane Alem, Bete Maryam, Bete Ammanuel and Bete Ghiorghis, dedicated to the Saviour of the World, the Virgin Mary, St Emmanuel, and St George, respectively, are free standing, joined to the rock only at their bases. Rising to eleven metres, more than thirty metres long and twenty metres wide, Medhane Alem is the largest of them all.

Isolated from the two, St George's has a striking cross-shaped form. A small baptismal pool nestles in a trench outside it. Inside, the atmosphere is cool and dark. Light shafts in through small windows. Cruciform columns attach themselves to the flat ceilings, supporting arches and dividing the space into aisles. Monolithic altars are a frequent element. The Selaissie Chapel has three altars, arranged side by side. Each flank of the central one is decorated with a cross and one beast of the Apocalypse: the man, the eagle, the bull and the lion. Niches and recesses have been carved into larger-than-life reliefs of saintly figures, identifiable by the nimbuses over their heads. However,

precise identities are unknown. A figure with a turban has invited particular interest. The inscription above him says 'St Cyriacus', but since he is devoid of a halo, and smaller than the others, his ostensible name has been doubted. One suggestion is that it could be an important clergyman, or even the Patriarch of Alexandria. Another enigmatic relief is that of a recumbent figure with wide shoulders and a featureless face. Depicted wearing a short tunic, hands crossed over the chest, he is popularly thought to be Jesus Christ.

As there are signs of stylistic differences amongst the churches, and their chronologies have not

Lalibela's churches have been hewn into the solid rock face.

been fully resolved, debate persists as to whether all of them were created during Lalibela's reign. Whatever the case may be, a tomb ascribed to him is tucked away under a cloth-covered altar in the depths of the church called Golgotha. While moss grows happily on the complex's 800 year old exteriors, religious services are conducted within as usual. And amongst the canonised of the Ethiopian Tewahedo Church is Lalibela, the man whose first nimbus, in a manner of speaking, was a swarm of bees.

The sunken church of Bete Ghiorghis.

Western Wall

Jerusalem, Israel

Ever since the organized existence of original Abrahamic religion, there has been only one temple. For Jews, it is simply the Temple. The Ark – a cupboard which contains the Torah (Hebrew Scriptures) – of every synagogue of the world looks towards Jerusalem, and in the city itself, every synagogue faces the Temple.

As the heart of the Biblical world, Jerusalem's stature as a holy city is unrivalled. In a period spanning roughly 2,000 years, defining events in this settlement at the northern edge of the Dead Sea, gave birth to some of the world's most revered sites. Many emblematic embryos of Judaism, Christianity, and Islam grew larger than life here. Ironically, this also

proved to be the bane of the 'City of Peace' (as its name translates from Hebrew). Coveted always by zealous forces of the three faiths, it was pounced upon, torn apart and wrested by each, as and when the balance of power shifed. Waves of Babylonians, Assyrians, Egyptians, Greeks, Romans, Persians, Arabs, Europeans and Turks swept across the city over 3,000 years. And during this time, the Temple was erected, felled, raised once more, only to be destroyed yet again.

Its genesis took place in around 1,000 BCE, with the conquest of Jerusalem by David. David's intention of creating a temple for the precious Ark of the Covenant, in which were kept the Ten Commandments given to Moses by God, was realized by his son

Facing page: *An orthodox Jew kisses the Wall in reverence.*

Following pages: *It is possible to discern between the Wall's original stones laid at the time of Herod, and those installed later, by the size and style in which they are chiselled.*

The wide plaza next to the Wall, overlooked by the Dome of the Rock, can hold prayer services and gatherings for thousands of people.

Solomon. Mount Moriah, later known as the Temple Mount, was chosen as the site. So was built what Jewish tradition refers to as the First Temple. Nebuchadnezzar's rampaging Babylonians brought it down in the sixth century BCE, which also coincided with the disappearance of the Ark – it hasn't been found since. The return from Babylon of the exiled Jews led to the building of the Second Temple, during the time of the prophets Ezra and Nehemiah.

In the first century CE, Judea was pulled into Rome's ever growing orbital fold. With Pontius Pilate watching over as Roman governor, the Jewish king Herod ruled Jerusalem. Not a popular ruler, the king is nevertheless referred to as Herod the Great; great because he

resurrected Jerusalem's architectural splendour. Amongst his edifices was the new, enlarged Second Temple. The Temple Mount had a successive series of four-sided enclosures, at the centre of which was the Holy of Holies, a room where the Ark was once housed. Only the High Priest was allowed into this innermost chamber. The outer constructions were great walls, of massive stones, some weighing up to 100 tons. Angered by Jewish revolts in the first century CE, the Roman general Titus razed the Temple to the ground. Only some of the walls were left standing. Of these, the Western Wall is believed to be closest to the site of the Holy of Holies. For the world's thirteen million Jews, it is now the most sacred place of worship.

Control of Jerusalem finally passed to Israel after the 1967 war with its Arab neighbours. The Wall, hemmed in by haphazard urban development, was given some breathing space. The suffocating residential sprawl was replaced by a wide, open plaza. Today, Jews from all over the world come to the Wall. They touch it in reverence. Many cry, mourning the lost Temple – thus also the name, the Wailing Wall. Clumps of vegetation sprout from cracks higher up, while in the crevices between the huge blocks of stone lower down, worshippers insert small slips of paper inscribed with prayers. Arks, stands, tables and chairs are ranged across the open floor for prayer. Ceremonies and rites are conducted by the Wall. Jewish boys are brought here to read from the Torah on the Sabbath after they perform the coming-of-age ritual of Bar-Mitzvah (son of the commandment) and Israeli soldiers are sworn to the protection of their country in its looming presence.

Their common prophetic heritage has meant that many religious places in the Holy Land bear Judaic, Christian and Islamic stamps. Though some Muslims consider the Western Wall the tethering site for the winged horse which took Muhammad to Jerusalem on his night rendezvous with Allah, the association is not emphasized. So this fragment of what once must have been a glorious temple remains virtually exclusive to Judaism. One day, they believe, the Messiah will come and raise the Third Temple.

In Jewish synagogues, Torah scrolls are stored in a cupboard-like container called the Ark – representing the Holy Ark of the Covenant – placed against a wall, a few feet above the floor.

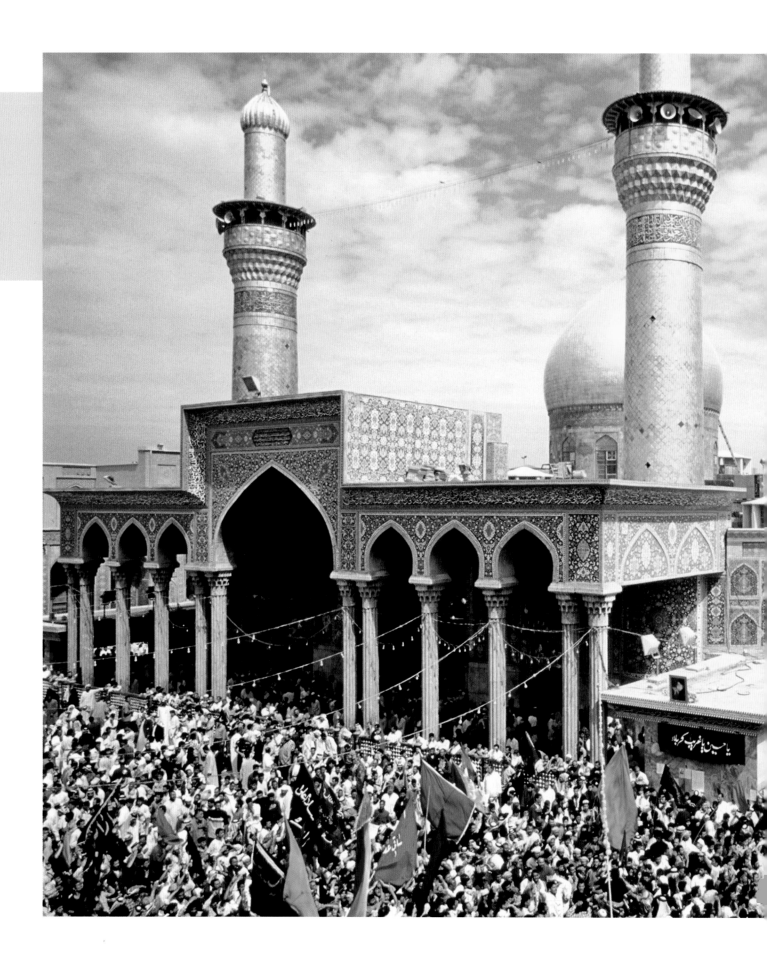

Masjid Al-Hussain
Karbala, Iraq

Upon the death of Muhammad in 632 CE, differences rose amongst his followers regarding the Prophet's rightful successor. This was to be the cause of the first and biggest schism in Islam, resulting in the split into Sunni and Shia sects. While the Sunnis pressed for an elected successor, the Shias favoured Muhammad's cousin and son-in-law (married to his daughter Fatima) Ali, on the grounds that he belonged to the Prophet's family. The former prevailed and Abu Bakr, one of the Prophet's earliest and closest comrades, was chosen as the first 'righteously guided' Caliph, or leader of the community. Almost twenty-five years and three caliphs down the line, Ali got his chance. As per the wishes of the majority, he became the fourth Caliph. Shias, however, hold him as Muhammad's first true successor, and the first Imam of the Ummah, or Muslim community. Unlike the Sunnis, they do not recognise the spiritual or political leadership of the Caliphate as it had originated.

Ali's rule as Caliph was plagued by civil wars. Amongst those who challenged him was Muawiyah, the powerful Governor of Syria. When Ali died, his followers automatically assumed his son Hassan as the next Caliph and second Imam. Hounded relentlessly by Muawiyah, Hassan was forced to formally relinquish

Facing page: *Thousands of Shia Muslims congregate at the shrine of Hussain, the third Imam.*

Muslim women relax under a beautifully decorated recessed arch.

the Caliphate to him. Believers in the bloodline of Muhammad and Ali, however, continued as such, and following Hassan's death, recognised his brother Hussain as the Caliph and third Imam. Meanwhile, Muawiyah was succeeded by his son Yazid I, who wished to retain the Caliphate. In order to do this unambiguously,

he had to decisively check the aspirations of Hussain and the Shias. Hussain's biggest following was in the Mesopotamian (Iraqi) town of Kufa. With a small entourage of family and armed companions, he began making his way across the desert to the town where he was promised sanctuary and support. Yazid's forces badgered him all along the way, until, finally, a few kilometres short of Kufa, the Caliph decided to conclude the issue once and for all. The stage was set for the Battle of Karbala. On one side stood Yazid's commanders at the head of several thousand soldiers. On the other were the Prophet's grandson and his small band of loyal fighters, perhaps no more than a hundred. Hopelessly outnumbered, Hussain and his warriors were slaughtered. For Shia Muslims, their burial places at Karbala are second in reverence only to Imam Ali's shrine at Najaf, also in Iraq.

Early Sunni rulers of the region, insecure about a significant Shia shrine in their midst, tried to curb its stature by discouraging pilgrims and destroying the buildings several times. However, from the eleventh century onwards, apart from a plundering raid by the Wahabis in the early nineteenth century, the shrine continued to grow in size and eminence.

The main Masjid-Al Hussain building stands over the grave of Hussain. It is prominent due to its pure gold covered dome, with twelve windows at the base, and two minarets, also bathed in gold. The Imam's tomb within is

decorated with precious metals, a silver screen and glass tiles. Apart from his grave are those of his two sons, Ali Akbar and the infant Ali Asghar; and close companion, Habib, who died fighting with him. The rest of his loyal Karbala 'army' is buried in a nearby mass grave. A boulevard connects this complex to another big shrine, that of Hussain's half-brother Abbas, who was also with him till he fell in battle.

Of special significance to the Shia community, and to Masjid Al-Hussain in particular, is Muharram, the first month of the Islamic calendar. The first ten days of this month are given to sorrowful remembrance of the tragic occurences at Karbala, 1300 years ago. Among the thousands of pilgrims which congregate at the shrine during this period are the elderly who hope to breathe their last at the doorstep of their Imam's final resting place. On Ashura, the tenth day of Muharram, Hussain's death is mourned with a final intensity. Gatherings called majilis are held at which the story of the martyrdom is retold in poetic verses. Theatrical re-enactments of the anguishing events are performed. Grief is expressed by beating the chest, and in an extreme emulation of the third Imam's suffering, wounds are inflicted by the pilgrims on themselves with knives and chains, while crying 'Ya Hussain!'

A Shia laments Hussain's death at Karbala in the traditional way by beating himself with chains.

Shrine of Saint Sarah
Saintes-Maries-de-la-Mer, France

In the first century CE, a ship left Egyptian shores, crossed the Mediterranean, and drifted on to the Camargue region of southern France. Aboard were Lazarus and the three Marys – Mary Salome, Mary Jacobe and Mary Magdalene, all close relatives or associates of Jesus Christ – fleeing persecution in the Holy Land. With them was Sarah, the Egyptian maid of Mary Jacobe. While the others continued further, Mary Salome, Mary Jacobe and Sarah stayed on at the desolate spot on the delta of the Rhone river. They died at their chosen home and were buried there. A small village, Saintes-Maries-de-la-Mer, came up around the spot. This is the story, as told in medieval Christian texts.

About a thousand years later, a group of war-affected people from India embarked on a westward journey. It was the beginning of a migration that would, over one more millennium, take them not only deep into the European continent, but also eventually across the Atlantic to the Americas. Though these people adopted the faiths of the regions they settled in, they were slow to let go of their ancestral Hindu beliefs. Their distinct ethnic and social identity too remained intact. They came to be known as the Romani, a people included later under the derogatory umbrella term 'gypsy'.

At some point in history, it is not clear when, the Romani discovered Sarah and adopted her

Facing page: A Romani woman touches St Sarah's clothes, in the traditional manner of paying homage.

The image of the dark Saint on way to ritual immersion, during the annual May festival.

as their patron saint. In their own tradition, she is believed to have been a royal Romani personage who was waiting to welcome and shelter the fleeing travellers in an unfamiliar land. However, this is difficult to corroborate historically, as the Romani did not penetrate France before the fifteenth century. Whatever be the case, Sarah was coloured with the hue of Kali, the wild, wrathful Hindu goddess, who was obviously alive in Romani religious consciousness at the time. Like Kali, she was depicted as dark, and called Saint Sara la Kali (in Sanskrit, the word 'Kali' means 'black female') – though, if one goes by Christian tradition, Sarah's dark exterior was a function of her Egyptian blood.

Pagan worship was performed at the site of Saintes-Maries-de-la-Mer Church, where Sarah is entombed, as early as the fourth century BCE. A little chapel to the Virgin Mary, established by the three Marys on their arrival, had grown into a small, fortified church by the ninth century. The relics of the founding ladies were recovered and re-interred in the fourteenth century. While the shrines of the two Marys are on the church floor, Sarah's is in a crypt below. Stiflingly warm, dimly lit and soot-blackened by candles over the years, it contains two altars, one pagan and one third-century Christian. Crowned and draped in skirts, Sarah's figure stands on the extreme right. Dusky of visage, she is, however, gentle-faced and

not fearsome like Kali. Romani worshippers come up to the plaster statue, murmur prayers, kiss the hem of her skirts, reach under her drapes to stroke her 'flesh', and then touch their lips to hers. Beside the image stands a wooden box full of letters thanking her for prayers answered, and oblations of crutches, braces and other items belonging to the sick who were cured with her blessings.

The other, more ebullient aspect of Sarah's worship is enacted during her May festival. A week before the actual day, Romani from near and far converge on Saintes-Maries-de-la-Mer. They pay their respects at her vault to the accompaniment of guitars and violins. On the final day, escorted by 'bodyguards' on white steeds, her statue, dressed

in new clothes, is carried on a wagon to the seashore for ritual submersion. It is a celebration of that fateful day when Sarah stood by the lapping waves guiding Jesus's kith and kin onto safe dry land. As the Saint's image is lowered and the edges of her skirts touch the water, the fervent masses fling themselves into the sea in the belief that at that very moment, the water has been shot with miraculous qualities. Far away in India, on the shores of the ancient Romani homeland, a similar immersion of the goddess Durga is carried out on her festival every year. It is perhaps no coincidence that one of the manifestations of Durga is Kali, who, sometime in the smoky past, contributed to the legend of St. Sarah.

Located in the dark womb of the church, St Sarah's crypt is illuminated by candles.

Qaraouine Mosque
Fez, Morocco

By the early eighth century, less than a hundred years after the Prophet's death, the heady boom of Islamic expansion was over. West of Mecca, Muslim suzerainty stretched over all of North Africa, and up into the Iberian Peninsula, known by the Arabs as Al-Andalus. In Morocco, home of the indigenous Berber people, the first independent Muslim kingdom was established by the Idrisids, who claimed descent from Ali, Muhammad's cousin and son-in-law. The city of Fez, in northern Morocco, became their capital. In the ninth century, refugees from the Tunisian city of Qaraouine came and settled in Fez. Amongst them were the sisters Fatima and Mariam. They inherited substantial wealth from their well-to-do trader father, and decided to spend most of it in building a mosque for their community. The Qaraouine Mosque, named after the city from where its sponsors came, was founded.

Over the centuries, as dynasties rose and fell, clashing with each other for dominance within the expanse of the Muslim world, the Mosque grew and increased in stature. Its first enhancement was in the tenth century, with the patronage of the Umayyad Caliphs, who ruled from their capital in Cordoba. The Mosque's overall area was increased considerably, and its original minaret was given a square shape, a style which was to be adopted for many minarets erected in mosques throughout North Africa. From the eleventh to

Facing page: The roof over one of the three ablution pools in the Mosque's oblong courtyard is held up by exquisite pillars and arches.

Another of the Mosque's ablution fountains set in the centre of beautiful mosaic flooring.

the thirteenth centuries, the Almoravids, and then the Almohades, ruled Morocco. The results of extensive reconstruction during this period prevail up to the present. Influences from the Great Mosque of Cordoba, built by the prolific Umayyads, are evident in the horseshoe arches and intricate geometric motifs and designs. Domes and vaults, embellishments in the form of Quranic calligraphy, water fountains, sundials and brass chandeliers were added at this time. So was the beautifully carved wooden minbar, or pulpit. The Saadi dynasty of the sixteenth and seventeenth centuries effected more renovations. Amongst them

are two attractive pavilions, where again, the influence from the great monuments of the Iberian Peninsula is evident – this time from Granada's Alhambra Palace.

Meanwhile, the mosque had evolved into the spiritual and intellectual centre of Moroccan Islam. It was no longer just a place of prayer but also one of higher learning. Chairs were established for scholars to impart the knowledge of the Quran, the Sharia and other religious and secular subjects. Amongst the brilliant minds who contributed to what is recognised as the oldest continuously functioning university in the world include the medieval Jewish philosopher-physician

Maimonides, the Arab genius Ibn Khaldun and the astronomer Al-Bitruji. In the fourteenth century, the mosque was endowed with a library. Over the years, its shelves swelled with valuable books and manuscripts. An original copy of Ibn Khaldun's *Al I'bar*; volumes of Imam Malik's *Al-Muwatta*, which are an early version of the Prophet's Hadith written on gazelle parchment; and a sixteenth-century Quran, presented by Ahmad Al-Mansur, the most illustrious of the Saadi sultans, are part of the collection.

Between the sloping green-tiled roofs of the mosque complex is the huge oblong sahn (courtyard). A large ablution fountain stands in the centre of the sahn, and two smaller ones are positioned under the graceful porticos protruding out of the galleries on either side. The first mihrab or pointer towards Mecca, denoted by a cedar wood screen, faces the courtyard. It is framed with zellij – handcrafted polychrome tiles arranged in intricate geometric patterns designed to evoke meditative and engrossed mindfulness. Behind it, rows of white-painted arches disappear into the cool darkness of the roofed innards. This is the main prayer hall. The ground is modestly covered with reed mats, and the ceilings are devoid of decoration. Over the main aisle, rise five domes, and in the deep recess of the forest-like interior, are the mihrab and the minbar. Lavishly decorated, they make up for the surrounding simplicity.

The Mosque's rich interior decoration includes zellij designs, with hexagons and six-pointed stars, and Kufic calligraphy.

Baha'i World Centre

Israel

In the early nineteenth century, Shaikh Ahmad, a religious leader from Iran, and then his successor, Sayyid Kazim, announced the imminent arrival of the Mahdi, the 'Guided One', the twelfth Shia Muslim Imam, who was prophesied to rescue strife-torn and debased humanity and restore peace, justice and goodness. The Shaikhis, as they were called, set about finding him. In the Iranian city of Shiraz, Kazim's disciple Mullah Hussain came into contact with one Sayyid Ali Muhammad. The young man from a business family claimed not only to be the immediate God-willed precursor to the Mahdi, but also a channel for revelation himself. Convinced by Muhammad's responses to their searching questions, Hussain, and

then others accepted his claim. Muhammad took the name 'the Bab' meaning 'the Gate'. As his following grew, so did his persecution by the Shia clergy and ruling class, who rejected his self-proclaimed status. The Bab was finally executed in 1850, in Tabriz.

One of the Bab's prominent and active supporters was Mirza Hussain Al-Nuri, the son of a high government official in the service of the Shah. Resented for his role in the death of the Bab, the Shah was subjected to a failed assassination attempt by the Babis. As a result, many Babis were rounded up, killed or imprisoned. Mirza Hussain, later known as Baha'u'llah, was one of those incarcerated in a Teheran dungeon. In the dismal depths of the underground prison

Facing page: *The Bab's tomb at Haifa, lit up at night.*

Nineteen terraces have been laid on the slopes of Mt Carmel, at the centre of which is the Bab's gold-domed tomb, overlooking Haifa Bay.

Baha'u'llah received divine visions informing him that he was the messianic Mahdi, whose coming was prophesied and preceded by the Bab. Eleven years later he declared this publicly. As was the case with the Bab, Baha'u'llah was a heretic in the eyes of the Shia rulers. He was driven out of Persia. His journey

precursor. Baha'u'llah's followers were known as Baha'is.

Baha'u'llah asserted that he was the culmination in a cycle that encompasses prophets, founders, and God-sent messengers of all religions, including, by implication, even of Buddhism and Hinduism. Baha'u'llah propagated the existence of one God, and that for the achievement of everlasting world harmony and order, this fact must be realised by humanity across the entire religious map of the world. Practically, towards this end, minimising economic disparity, ensuring universal education and equal status for men and women must be strived for.

Though Baha'u'llah designated only two holy sites – the Bab's and his own house, at Shiraz and Baghdad, respectively – prevailing circumstances in those countries make them almost impossible to visit. However, the places of significance scattered across the two north-western Israeli cities of Haifa and Acre, constitute the present nine-day Baha'i pilgrimage. Clubbed together, they are known as the Baha'i World Centre. In 1909, as per the directions of Baha'u'llah, the Bab's remains were entombed on the slope of the historic Mount Carmel at Haifa. Over the years, with the expertise of renowned architects, the plain hillside was transformed into a remarkable development. Today, nineteen beautiful terraces of manicured grass, fringed with wilder flora, extend for one kilometre up to the top of the slope. At the centre of this trail of garden landings is

the nine-roomed mausoleum. Designed in a fusion of Eastern and Western styles, it has an octagonal dome overlaid with fire-glazed gold leaf tiles. The four corners of the exterior are embellished with the Greatest Name of God, in the signature Baha'i calligraphy. Inside, on the walls, hangs the Tablet of Visitation, the Baha'i's dearest prayer. Arranged in an arc on the hillside are the striking buildings of the International Teaching Centre; the Seat of the Universal House of Justice, which is the faith's apex governing body; the Centre for the Study of the Texts; and the International Archives. The whole ensemble looks northeast, across Haifa Bay, for in this direction lies Acre, site of the most holy Baha'i shrine.

Baha'u'llah came to Acre in 1868 as a prisoner. His cell is part of the pilgrimage. So is the house in Mazra'a, on the outskirts, where he stayed for two years, and the house known as the Mansion of Bahji, where he spent the last thirteen years of his life. He was buried next to the latter. His last resting place is simple – a small entombment room in a little garden entered through a low gate. The Greatest Name emblem is emblazoned on the triangular gable of the porch. A chandelier adorns its ceiling. Outside, the much bigger gardens are studded with another Baha'i symbol, the nine-pointed star. Nine is a vital number in the Baha'i worldview of converging religions. As the final single digit, it represents fulfillment and completeness.

finally ended in the Palestinian town of Acre, where he died in 1892. By this time he had been recognised by the overwhelming majority of Babis as the foretold Imam. By virtue of this, his was a new religion that superseded that of the Bab's, who continued to be regarded as its highly revered

Shwedagon Pagoda
Yangon, Myanmar

An array of glittering shrines, pavilions and prayer halls profusely strew the Shwedagon compound.

Theravada or the 'Teaching of the Elders' Buddhism is the more conservative of the two main branches – the other being Mahayana or the 'Greater Vehicle'. Theravada claims to remain true to the Buddha's original doctrine. Its emphasis is on striving to attain Enlightenment and freedom from the cycle of life and death by introspection and following the Buddha's teachings, without resorting to esoteric rituals. Theravada came into its own in Myanmar with King Anawrahta, who first unified the country's miscellaneous kingdoms in the eleventh century. Shwedagon Pagoda or Stupa evidently existed much before this. Buddhist tradition places its founding as contemporaneous with the

A monk meditates facing Shwedagon, the most sacred site for Myanmarese Buddhists. Besides hairs of the Buddha, the Pagoda is said to enshrine other relics described in Buddhist texts.

Buddha's lifetime. It records that during the reign of King Ukkalapa, two brothers travelled to India and brought back four strands of the Buddha's hair. These were enshrined in a stupa on Singuttara hill, at present-day Yangon. Not much is known of the Stupa's fate up to the fifteenth century. At this time, with the patronage of Queen Shin Sawboo, the compound was enlarged and beautified, ancillary constructions added, and the attendant manpower increased considerably. Significantly, the Queen had the Pagoda overlaid with gold equalling her own bodyweight. Her successor, King Dhammazedi, added another, much more generous dose of the yellow metal, amounting to four times his

own weight plus that of his wife's. From then, though the Pagoda suffered earthquakes and British colonial occupation, its dazzling demeanour continued to grow.

Stairways through four gates lead up to the surrounding marble platform. Stepping onto it, one is struck by the striking mountain of gold soaring into the sky. Ringed with smaller stupas at the plinth level, the Pagoda ascends through different sections. Square terraces give way via octagonal sections to the circular body. The bell-like trunk is embellished with flowery motifs. Above it the shape tapers into the symbolic upturned alms bowl of the Buddhist ascetic. This is followed by a row each of down-turned and upturned lotus petals,

and then the 'banana bud' section. Though every square inch of the immensity is swathed with gold leaf and plates, the greatest treasures are encrusted on the seven-tiered spire. These consist of several thousand diamonds, rubies and other precious stones. The Stupa climaxes with a single seventy-six-carat diamond on its tip.

Below, the wide platform is littered with a plethora of shrines and prayer halls. Carved woodwork on some depicts scenes from the Buddha's life. Buddha images are everywhere. They include the individually standing First, Second and the historical Buddhas; a series of twenty-eight previous incarnations; and another in the reclining posture. A banyan tree,

born from the sap of the original Bodhi Tree, grows in a corner. The Stupa's origins are recalled at the statue of Ukkalapa and at the Hair Relics Well, where the sacred hair were washed before enshrinement.

Unlike Mahayana Buddhism, Theravada is non-inclusive of gods and supernatural beings in the pursuit of Enlightenment. Despite this, it was unable to shut its doors to them completely in the face of Myanmar's co-existing religions. The Shwedagon Pagoda displays those influences. Nats are spirit deities whose worship predates the advent of Buddhism in Myanmar. They have their own hierarchy, which runs up from lower spirits that represent trees, water, and so on, to a pantheon of Great Nats.

Gold is the prevailing colour at Shwedagon. Apart from covering the main stupa, it is ubiquitous on the buildings, ornamentation and numerous statues of the Buddha.

The exalted Shwedagon is watched over by its own glass-encased guardian Nat, as well as by the King of Nats. Similarly an astrological system derived from Hinduism manifests as eight stations coinciding with the days of the week – Wednesday has two, demarcated into a.m. and p.m. – ranged around the Stupa. Each day has a designated planet and an animal icon. These are represented at the stations, along with images of a guardian spirit and a Buddha. Prayers are offered by people at particular stations consonant with their day of birth.

It is believed that miracles are possible if the Wonder-Working Buddha statue wills, and wishes may be granted by praying to the great Stupa from a star-shaped spot.

An image in the Izza Gawna pavilion speaks of a miracle which resulted in a monk regaining his vision by transplanting the eyes of a bullock and a goat. Besides the golden bells that adorn the heights of the tall Pagoda, are the forty-ton Maha Tissada and the twenty-ton Maha Gandha bells. The latter was appropriated by the British and sent to India, but it proved too much to handle and fell into the river. Figuring its retrieval was impossible, the British declared it 'given back'. Unwilling to give their treasure up, however, Myanmarese divers fastened it with bamboo shafts, buoyed it up to the surface, and restored it to the foot of Shwedagon – a feat almost miraculous in itself.

Above: *Mythical lions guard the way to a small shrine.*

Facing page: *Though Shwedagon is a Theravada monument, the influence of local and other religious elements is evident in the images of supernatural beings co-existing with the Buddha's images.*

Stonehenge
England

The Celts were a group of various tribes, bound by a common linguistic family, that proliferated in western, central and parts of southern and eastern Europe, during the Iron Age. Celtic religion brimmed with gods and goddesses associated with natural elements as well as human occupations. The custodians of this religion were the druids. Priests, certainly, they were also holders of great knowledge and wisdom gained over many years of rigorous learning.

Stonehenge was built, abandoned, enhanced, rearranged and used over fifteen hundred years, from c. 3100 BCE to 1600 BCE. At various times, it functioned as a cemetery and a place of Celtic religious rituals, though the manner in which the latter were conducted is unclear. Essentially, the site is a formation of concentric circles, with an overall diameter of about 110 metres. Many of the constructions of mud, timber and towering rocks are now gone but there is ample evidence of the ensemble as it once existed on the Salisbury Plain. The outermost ring comprises a ditch and a mud bank immediately inside it, an arrangement which, it is argued, does not qualify it as a true henge, wherein the order of the two features is reversed. (A small bank on the outside has, however, been discerned). This external boundary is broken by two main entrances, of which the northeastern is the largest. The Aubrey Holes, empty pits that may have once contained timber posts, form the next circle.

Facing page: Sarsen rocks, made of sandstone and silica, have been used in Stonehenge's megalithic architecture. Each can weigh up to twenty-five tons or more – as much as five to six elephants.

Modern druids conduct a ceremony at the altar stone. There are thousands of practicing druids in Britain, belonging to various orders. Dressing in robes and wearing ancient Celtic symbols is part of their ceremonial rituals.

Further in are two more rounds of unendowed holes, and then the prodigious wonders of Stonehenge.

The incomplete circle of Sarsen stones comes first. It was once composed of thirty upright stones, each over four metres high and two metres wide. Considering that they weigh about twenty-five tons each, transporting them from their quarry forty kilometres away would have been a remarkable feat. The uprights are bridged by lintel stones connected to each other with tongue and groove joints. All the stones are shaped to impart a constant vertical and circular perspective. Ten more Sarsens and lintels, this time structured into five trilithons, were installed within, relative to each other according to size. Their magnitudes were even more impressive: the largest individual stone protruded seven metres above the ground and is estimated to have tipped the scales at fifty tons. Very little of this great formation survives.

Stonehenge's inner curvatures include two crescents of about eighty stones, of which half were bluestones. Relatively much lighter, these four-ton boulders were hauled in, possibly by a combination of overland and riverine route, from their place of origin, also many kilometres away. At the centre of Stonehenge's annuli is the recumbent Altar Stone. Free-standing monoliths occupy other spots in the larger space. One of these is the Heel stone, embedded outside the large circle in the Avenue, a distinct causeway leading to the Avon river a few kilometres away. Legend has it that the Devil hurled the massive rock at a friar, whose heel it struck, thereby acquiring its name.

By the early part of the first millennium CE, the all-devouring Roman Empire and surging Germanic hordes had all but erased Celtic culture off the map. The druids passed on, leaving virtually no record of their enigmatic existence. They popped up in later Irish folklore, but it was only in the Romantic age of the seventeenth and eighteenth centuries that there was a significant revival of popular interest in their long-lost practices. The Ancient Order of the Druids was floated in 1781, and momentum picked up in the twentieth century with the sprouting of a host of groups professing their own distinct brands of neo-Druidism. None of these credibly derive from ancient druidry, as in the absence of historical corroboration, that world remains a figment of speculation. Rather than religious doctrine, the emphasis of modern druidry is on achieving universal harmony, peace and healing through reverence of nature, and respect for ancestors and their traditions.

The mysticism of Stonehenge was reaffirmed after three thousand years of disregard. In 1905, the Ancient Order of Druids conducted

the first modern ceremony in its portals. Since then Druidic, neo-pagan and New Age groups have been permitted limited ritual use of the site. The big occasions are the summer and winter solstices. On these days modern druids gather beside the silent stones in the darkness before dawn. Some wear robes and carry staffs, replicating what they believe were the vestments of their ancient predecessors. An altar is created on the grass and objects symbolic of the elements placed on it. Worshippers hold hands around the altar in a circle, chant, sip sacralised water and express gratitude and love for the spirits of nature, joyously welcoming the rays of the rising sun on the staggering silhouettes of Stonehenge.

View of the layout and construction of Stonehenge's inner circles. Prominent are the three-piece megaliths with a lintel joining two erect rocks.

Uluru

Australia

In the beginning, the world was plain and formless. Then began the Dreaming. Fantastic beings, resembling humans and animals, who had lain dormant beneath its surface, emerged and became restless. They travelled the wide continent, camped, fought, hunted, dug, conducted ceremonies and generally did all the things normal to everyday life. Eventually, they tired and retreated back to their abodes. Wherever they had gone, however, they had left evidences of their activities. These were in the form of natural features like rivers, trees, caves, mountains and rocks. So the world was shaped. One of its features was Uluru, a gargantuan mass of arkose sandstone.

Uluru (also called Ayers Rock) thrusts out in solitary splendour from the arid flatness of the central Australian desert. About 350 metres high and nine-and-a-half kilometres in circumference, it is more a mountain than a rock. At sunrise and sunset, its visage is particularly entrancing due to the red hue imparted by the play of light on the rock's mineral content. Geologists attribute Uluru's orgins to mountains that were formed as part of an alluvial fan – a geographical feature created by rivers emerging onto the plains and breaking into channels, thereby depositing ridges of sand. Slowly, the softer rock around Uluru eroded, while the hard lump persisted.

In the Indigenous Australian peoples's (also known as Aborigines) tradition, the Dreaming or Dreamtime was a period in the

Facing page: Beyond the immediate vicinity of the rock stretches the inhospitable Australian outback.

There are more than forty named Anangu sacred sites, and eleven Dreaming trails in the vicinity of Uluru and a cluster of similar rocks called Kata Tjuta, twenty-five kilometres away.

remote past. Occurrences during Dreamtime form the basis of their religious and secular life. They consider their customs to be a reflection of those practiced by their 'founding' ancestors. Their sites of veneration are directly connected with events that took place as a result of their ancestors's amazing deeds. Amongst the many Aboriginal stories regarding the genesis of Uluru is one concerning a great feast at which the host tribes waited but the invitees did not turn up: their attentions had been captured by the alluring Sleepy Lizard Women. The result was a tragic battle between the irate hosts and their irresponsible guests in which the leaders of both sides were killed. In grief, the earth erupted as Uluru.

Uluru's environs are littered with dozens of places sacred to their ancient owners, the Anangu, one of the indigenous groups of the continent. Some of these places are shown to visitors. Others are secret, frequented only by the Anangu. Though the rock itself is utterly bald, its rain runoff nurtures a flourishing ecosystem of vegetation, water bodies and wildlife. A pool is the home of the Dreamtime water snake, Wanampi. Shallow caves at the base are carved and painted with human and animal figures, and unfathomable symbols. Ancient in origins, the art has undergone routine renovation through the ages, as the site has continued to be used for rituals. Bowl-shaped hollows on the inclines are explained as the scrabble marks left by Tatji, the small red lizard, as he tried in vain to prise out his throwing stick from the rock. Another story immortalised in rock is of the fight between the Bell-Bird brothers and Mita and Lungkata, two blue-tongued lizard men, over an emu: a cracked stone slab is the leftover hunk of the bird's meat. When the raging Bell-Bird brothers incinerated the lizard men's home, the latter tried to get away by scampering up the rock. But they fell into the fire and perished. The gray lichen which appears on the rock face due to moisture represents the smoke from the fire, and two boulders, the corpses of the unfortunate reptilians.

The wanderings of the legendary Dreaming life-forms across the endless Australian landscape are represented as well-defined trails. Discernible usually only to the Aborigines, they are tracked by songlines. Amongst other things, songlines can be described as a primeval navigational system, comprising singing, storytelling and art, performed while the Aborigines walk the trails. Complex song cycles, as they unfold, inform the way to the sacred places. Songline trails often span the territories of different clans and, consequently, a single song cycle can be made up of different languages. Up and across Uluru, too, there are songline trails.

Because of its sacred nature, the Anangu do not encourage visitors to ascend the rock. However, though they are the owners, the lease is with the Australian government, and there is no official ban on climbing. On the contrary, a route, made easier with a chain-link fence, has been set up for climbers. The fact that the route also cuts across a songline trail does not please the Anangu. Over the years, tourists have picked up pieces of Uluru and taken them home as souvenirs, only to have returned them later, anonymously, by mail. Since the acquisition, all contended, their luck had turned for the worse.

Over thousands of years, rain water flows have carved hollows on the rock face.

Jokhang Temple
Lhasa, Tibet

Tantra emerged as a cult within the existing Hindu and Buddhist religious traditions of India in the fifth century. Broadly, it holds that the gross universe is a manifestation of divine energies which must be harnessed and sublimated, rather than shut out, to realise, not just spiritual, but also material objectives. Geared towards this end, Tantric practices are a complex and often intertwined mélange of esoteric rituals, worship of deities, yoga, magical rites, mantras and symbols. Tantra curled onto Mahayana Buddhism, and a combination of the two split away as Vajrayana or the 'Thunderbolt Vehicle'.

This limb reached out northward in the eighth century. At its tip was Padmasambhava, a monk who made his way from the snows of Kashmir to plant Vajrayana on the 'Roof of the World'. Buddhism was already squarely in place in these high altitude deserts. It had been established as the official religion of the Tibetan Empire a hundred years ago by King Tsongsän Gampo, and promoted by no mean contributions from his two Buddhist wives. Also in place was Bon, the original animistic and shamanistic religion of Tibet, dating from misty antiquity far before the birth of the Buddha. Padmasambhava's Thunderbolt embedded itself into both. The result was Tibetan Buddhism.

Tsongsän Gampo had two queens. Weng Chen was Chinese, and Bhrikuti, Nepalese. Both were Buddhist. As part of their dowries they brought with them a host of Buddhist statues and objects of religious significance. Of these, the

Facing page: *The image of Sage Padmasambhava, who brought Vajrayana Buddhism into Tibet.*

statues of Akhshobya Vajra (eight-year-old Buddha) and the Jowo Sakyamuni (twelve-year-old Buddha) were considered especially sacred. Two temples were built to house these statues. The Ramoche temple was located on a site under which a sacred lake was believed to exist. In it was placed the Jowo Sakyamuni image. Akshobya Vajra was ensconced in the Rasa Trulnang Tsuglag Khang, now known as Jokhang. Later events resulted in a swap of locations.

Jowo Sakyamuni, enshrined in Jokhang, is the most revered Buddhist image in Tibet. Regarded as a creation of Vishvakarma, the Hindu god of artists and craftsmen, it was presented by the king of Magadha in eastern India to the Tang emperor, who was Weng Chen's father. The magnificent one-and-half-metre-tall statue and its accoutrements, in the central chamber, are fashioned from precious metals and studded with gems. In the front is a row of burning butter lamps.

There are many rooms in the massive four-storeyed temple. Each has its own image, including that of Padmasambhava, the original master. Tsongsän Gampo's idol is accompanied with those of his wives on either side. The two women illustrate the primordial feminine principles that crept into Buddhism

from Tantra. While one of the royal ladies is portrayed as Green Tara, the protectress, the other is shown as White Tara, the compassionate. The king, held to be a manifestation of Avalokiteswara – as is the Dalai Lama, Tibet's religious and temporal head – the Buddha of Compassion (known in Tibet as Chenrezig), is depicted as such.

The building's layout is an architectural blend of the Indian vihara or monastery, and Nepalese and Tang Chinese styles. The Dharmachakra or the Wheel of Law, flanked by figures of two deer, stands outside on the temple's gilted roof. One animal represents the Buddha's landmark first sermon, and the other, the deer park, where

it was delivered. The Jokhang's hallowed precincts are the focus of three circumambulatory orbits. The outermost, its eight-kilometre route surviving now only in fragments, takes the whole city in its ambit. The middle path winds for almost a kilometre through the surrounding sacred district, lined with bazaars. Once, its four cardinal corners were marked with large incense burners. The innermost is within the temple itself. As per Buddhist custom, pilgrims complete these encirclements in a clockwise direction, murmuring mantras, spinning prayer wheels, prostrating themselves and praying.

A painting of Buddha inside Jokhang, which itself means 'House of the Buddha'.

Varanasi
India

The Ganga is born out of glacial melt in the high Himalayan mountains. From its source at Gangotri to its assimilation in the Bay of Bengal, it winds 2,500 kilometres through northern India. Along with its tributaries, the river is a sustainer of life on the Indo-Gangetic plains. According to the myth associated with her birth, Ganga was a divine maiden formed out of the water of the gods. King Bhagiratha prayed to Brahma, the Hindu God of Creation, to send her down on earth to wash clean the cursed spirits of his ancestors. On the Creator's command, Ganga descended from heaven, but with her full might. Anticipating catastrophic devastation, Shiva, the God of Destruction, took the brunt of her force on his matted locks, and allowed her to stream out as a gentler, bountiful flow, purifying all that she touched. Rivers are generally venerated in Hinduism but the Ganga is by far the holiest of them all.

Among the towns that lie on the Ganga's banks is Varanasi. One of the oldest continuously inhabited cities of the world, Varanasi is first mentioned in the *Rig Veda*, Hinduism's earliest scripture, compiled in c. 1,500 BCE. The Buddha gave his first sermon at Sarnath, near Varanasi in the sixth century BCE. In the eleventh century, the Muslim invaders Mahmud of Ghazni and Muhammad Ghori wreaked havoc on the city. During the Mughal period, though Varanasi benefited

Facing page: *Hindus believe that a dip in the Ganga remits sins. For many residents of Varanasi this is a routine affair, while others make the pilgrimage from across the expanse of the country.*

A festive evening in the City of Lights

from Emperor Akbar's constructive energies, under his great grandson Aurangzeb, some structures were again destroyed.

The city's name comes from two small streams, the Varuna and the Assi, which join with the Ganga here. It is also called Kashi, the 'City of Lights', for its attraction to the seekers of truth. The faithful flock here to take a dip in the river, which is believed to cleanse them of all sins, and free them from the endless cycle of life and death – a fundamental philosophical tenet in Hinduism.

The Ganga's western banks at Varanasi are lined with ghats, which are designated areas for activities linked to the river. These are mostly constructed embankments with steps leading up from the lapping waters. Possibly as many as a hundred ghats, many of which have existed for hundreds of years, extend over more than five kilometres along the river. Much of the city's religious business is conducted on them. The ghats are riddled with temples and shrines, including those dedicated to the Goddess Ganga. Many claim independent legendary origins; several have their own festivals and pilgrimages. They are sites of sculptures, old buildings, the odd mosque, and even an astronomical observatory built in the eighteenth century by the ruler of Jaipur. Some ghats are populated by members of specific regions like Bengal, South India, and Nepal, others by particular communities like oil-pressers, boatmen and washerfolk.

Ascetic sects like the Juna and the Naga have rights over their own ghats, while traditional wrestlers practise their sport on others. At various periods of history, different ghats have been the favourite haunts of specific saints, scholars, and philosophers.

The row of ghats begins from Assi in the south. Some are accorded more prominence than others. Harishchandra and Manikarnika have the most sombre function. They are cremation sites, especially favoured by devout Hindus for their final rites. Imagined as the meeting point of five sacred rivers, the Panchaganga ghat is considered especially sacred. At sunrise and sunset, this riverside segment is set alight with aarti, a prayer ritual performed with oil lamps and hymns. Dashashwamedha ghat is perhaps the most famous of all. The story goes that Brahma performed the meritorious ten-horse sacrifice on its sacred ground. Ritual fire worship is conducted here in the evenings.

Varanasi is regarded as one of the homes of Shiva. It is one of the several Shaktipeeths scattered across the country. Legend says that when, at the death of his wife Shakti, an enraged Shiva launched into the dance of destruction with her head in his hands, Vishnu, the God of Preservation, was compelled to use his disc to shatter the head. The places where the pieces landed are called Shaktipeeths. Varanasi is also one of Hinduism's twelve Jyotirlingams, the most revered of all the sites where Shiva's phallus

An astrologer attends customers on the ghats of the sacred stream.

symbol or lingam is worshipped. In the City of Lights it is enshrined in the age-old Vishwanath temple. Last rebuilt in 1780 by the central Indian queen Ahilyabai, the building's spires were plated with one ton of gold, by Ranjit Singh, the 'Lion King' of Punjab, in the nineteenth century. Insulated within the middle of the shrine complex is the Gyan Vapi well. It is believed that during Muslim invasions in the medieval period, the lingam of Vishwanath, the 'Lord of the World', was consigned to its depths for safekeeping.

Ghats along the river are a melee of boats, pilgrims, ancient temples and homes. The American author Mark Twain (1835-1910) wrote, "Benares (Varanasi) is older than history, older than tradition, older even than legend, and looks twice as old as all of them put together."

Haeinsa Temple
Gaya Mountains, South Korea

In the fifth century, an Indian monk, Bodhidharma, came to China with a form of Buddhism, which came to be called Chan (Zen in Japanese, Seon in Korean). A development out of the Mahayana school, this doctrine distanced itself from scriptural learning and emphasised the importance of personal experience through meditation. After all, it asserted, this was how the Buddha had himself attained Enlightenment. Later, tradition says, he had conveyed this way speechlessly through the Flower Sermon, where it was grasped by only one of his disciples, Mahakasyapa.

From Bodhidharma began a line of Six Patriarchs of Chan, the last of which was Huineng. Huineng's disciples imparted the philosophy and its methods to Korean monks. The Nine Mountain Schools, the initial Seon monasteries, were established by the ninth century, and from the tenth to the fourteenth centuries, Seon thrived under the Goryeo kings. During this time also, various Seon schools were united into the Jogye Order. Jogye weathered a period of decline in the intervening centuries to emerge eventually as the most widely practiced form of Buddhism in Korea.

Buddhist tradition holds precious the Three Jewels. They are: the Buddha himself, the Dharma or his teachings, and the Sangha, or the monastic community.

Facing page: *A Buddhist monk beats a ceremonial drum as a call to prayer at the Haeinsa Temple.*

Haeinsa is most famous for being the repository of the Korean Tripitaka canon, which it has housed for hundreds of years.

'Taking refuge' in these, by following recommended guidelines and practices, is desirable for the faithful. Korea's Jogye Order is organised into twenty-four head temples. Amongst them are the Three Jewel Temples, each standing for one of the 'refuges'. Of these, Haeinsa represents the Dharma. The shrine's origins are attributed to a miracle whereby chantings of local monks caused a ninth-century queen to be cured of a deadly tumour. Not much is known of the temple during its first seven hundred years or so of existence. The most significant of its buildings, a repository, was raised in the fifteenth century. It was the only structure that survived an inferno in 1817, which almost totally consumed the rest of the wooden complex on Mount Kaya.

Collectively, the early Buddhist scriptures are known as the Tripitakas. For many years they were passed down orally. Most early inscriptions were lost during the geographical spread of Buddhism. The oldest and most complete of the surviving works date back to the thirteenth century. At this time the Koreans were fighting the Khitan Mongols, and the rulers commissioned the writings in the belief that this would prove auspicious in turning the tide in their favour. At the end of twelve years, the yield from this mammoth project was a corpus of Tripitakas carved in Chinese on no less than 81,000 wooden blocks, organized in more than 6,800 volumes. Birch wood used for this epic creation was specially cured by immersion in sea water, and then by drying under shade over a process that lasted several years. The edges of the pieces were lacquered with metal as a precaution against warping. Each block was numbered and titled. It is notable that even over such a vast scale, the character style is so consistent that it does not appear to be the handiwork of many different people. The blocks are as much an aesthetic heritage as a technical achievement.

The repositories in which they are stored are no less scientifically remarkable. The four buildings escaped the fire because they were set apart from the temple complex, on the highest point of the site. They were designed with the conscious objective of preserving their valuable contents for posterity. To ensure adequate ventilation and prevent humidity from exceeding ideal levels, the windows are calculatedly positioned, slatted and of different sizes. Equal attention has been given to the floor and the ceiling. Below the earthen surface of the former is a porous layer of charcoal which regulates moisture, and the clay and wooden rafters attached to the tiled roof are resistant to abrupt changes in temperature. In this climate-controlled archive, the evenly cut blocks are neatly packed in rows of shelves.

Several hundred monks live and practice their meditative religion at Haeinsa, the 'Temple of Reflections on a Smooth Sea'.

They reflect upon their thoughts at the Vairochana or Universal Buddha image in the Great Hall of Light and Silence. The Vairochana represents emptiness. Its doctrine is elaborated in the Mahavairochana Sutra, a rendering of which may be found ensconced nearby in a place safe and silent, but far from empty.

The contemplative atmosphere in one of the Temple's several prayer rooms.

Harmandir Sahib

Amritsar, India

The Sikh religion began in the fifteenth century as a social reform movement, incorporating clear concepts of divinity. The social message was one of egalitarianism in the context of the caste-ridden Hindu society. A strong work ethic, and commitment to worldly duties, as opposed to reclusiveness, was advocated. This included protection of, and charity towards, the downtrodden. On the religious plane, Sikhism (the word comes from 'shishya', Sanskrit for 'pupil') preached the existence of one genderless and formless God, unity with whom is possible without rituals, through personal devotion, and the Sikh way of life.

Nanak, the founder of the faith, was the son of high-caste Hindu parents of Punjab, a region covering parts of North India and Pakistan. He was followed by a line of nine more saints or Gurus (teachers), the last of who was Gobind Singh (d.1708). As its adherents increased, the Mughal government of the time became nervous of a growning alternate centre of power within Sikhism's dominions. The resulting conflict contributed to the organisation of the Sikh community into a formidable military force. By the first half of the nineteenth century, they had gained control over the whole of Punjab, as well as Kashmir.

During the time of Amar Das, the third Guru, his successor-to-be, Ram Das, took up residence next to a small jungle spring, the waters of which were reputed to have

Facing page: Harmandir Sahib is a blend of Hindu and Islamic architecture. Its foundation stone was laid by a Muslim saint Hazrat Mian Mir, on the invitation of the fifth Sikh Guru, in 1588. The Temple was completed in 1601.

healing powers. Ram Das and his followers enlarged the small pool and called it Amritsar, the 'Tank of Nectar'. Soon, a town of the same name sprouted around it. The fifth Guru, Arjan Dev, erected a temple in the middle of this tank, and in it was installed a compilation of the sayings of the first five Gurus. This was the Adi Granth, the first version of the Granth Sahib, the holy book of the Sikhs. The temple, called Harmandir Sahib or the 'Temple of God', was promoted as the epicentre of the Sikh religion.

Today, Harmandir Sahib stands in the middle of a huge square-shaped complex made of white marble. Its four portals symbolise Sikhism's openness to members of all religions, communities and castes. One passes through the Darshani Deorhi archway and walks to the temple via a causeway. Gilded with gold leaf, the resplendent three-storeyed structure is crowned with an inverted lotus-shaped dome. The lavish embellishment – due to which it is popularly known as the

Golden Temple – was provided by Ranjit Singh, architect of the Sikh Empire. The interiors are decorated with sculpted wooden panels, intricate gold and silver ornamentation, frescoes and stained glass. Gobind Singh had decreed that after him the Granth Sahib should be revered as the eternal Guru. Laid on a throne on the ground floor below a jewelled canopy, the book is read aloud continuously by priests.

West of the golden shrine is the five-storeyed Akal Takht, the supreme spiritual and temporal seat of the Sikh religion. Built in the early seventeenth century, this was where the Gurus held court and issued their commandments, and from where today, religious writs for the community continue to be passed. Every night, the Granth Sahib is brought to 'rest' at the Akal Takht. In the wee hours of morning, it is taken back to Harmandir Sahib in a silver and gold palanquin.

Besides the inner circumambulation of the temple,

The Temple, lit up for the Baisakhi festival. On all days, the reciting of hymns begins in the wee hours and ends late at night. The reading of the Granth Sahib, however, continues non-stop at various locations in the complex.

pilgrims do the customary walk around the tank on a wide pathway. Along the way, there are lesser shrines and sites associated with the temple's history. Amongst them is the Dukh Banjani ber (jujube) tree, which is said to have marked the little pool when Guru Amar Das first discovered it. A second tree of the same species on the northern bank gave shade to Baba Buddha, the first head priest, as he supervised the construction of the temple. Yet another hardy specimen growing near the Darshani Deorhi sheltered Arjan Dev, and Mehtab Singh, a warrior who rode all the way from Rajasthan to face-off with Massa Rangar, the local Muslim chieftain who dared to occupy the sacred precincts. Bathing at a spot named Athsath Tirath is considered equal to visiting sixty-eight Hindu shrines of India. Directly across, one can see a flight of steps leading down to the water from the glittering walls of the Golden Temple. Standing there, pilgrims scoop up a handful of the holy water, and sprinkle it on their heads.

Left: *A ritual dip in the holy tank, the origins of which lie in a small spring.*

Facing page: *A priest reads the Granth Sahib. The book consists of verses by Sikh Gurus, Muslim and Hindu saints, and other spiritually inclined personalities. The second, and final, version of the book was completed in the early eighteenth century.*

Maori Meeting Places
New Zealand

Sometime before the thirteenth century, the Maori (meaning 'ordinary'), a Polynesian people, crossed the south Pacific Ocean in big, robust canoes and landed on the shores of New Zealand. There is no evidence of human habitation on the islands preceding their arrival. They established settlements, fought wars, practiced farming and a religion rooted in the culture of their original home. Though with the coming of the Europeans in the eighteenth century most Maori converted to Christianity, their indigenous belief system is very much alive, albeit layered with missionary faith.

Maori gods represent natural phenomena and all living things. Io, the one with no beginning or end, is supreme. The other great gods are the offspring of Ranginui, Lord of the Skies, and Papatuanaku, the Earth Goddess. Tangaroa created the sea, Tawhirimatea, the wind and storms. Tumataunega brought war, Rongo agriculture, and Whiro cast darkness and evil. From Tane, he of the forests, and Hinetitama, a woman, emanated the human race. Therefore gods are not just supernatural rulers but also ancestors. This is the basis of Maori social organisation and religion. Precise genealogical lineages are traced back from the family level, through sub-tribes and tribes, right up to the first canoes. Connection to one's forefathers is a Maori's social identity. Ancestors, both immediate and from generations extending deep into the dim mists

Facing page: *Depictions of ancestors outside Te Aronui, one of New Zealand's few fully-carved meeting houses.*

The figure of a highly regarded ancestor crowns the façade of a meeting house.

Facing page: Queen Victoria's statue, in the protective shade of a meeting house structure, is an indicator of the historic engagement of Maori culture with New Zealand's white population.

of time, are not just revered but occupy a palpable and fundamental presence in everyday life and customs.

The focus of Maori community life is the meeting house, variously called whare hui, whare rununga and whare whakairo. It is where the highest mana or spiritual essence – also present in tohungas or priests – resides. Mana is shielded and shrouded by tapu, a strict web of sacred rules and restrictions. Flouting tapu is taboo and can lead to degrees of reprimand and misfortune; in earlier times it could be punishable by death. Tapu concerns the personal, such as the ban on ordinary persons to approach or feed a priest, as well as objects and buildings. The whare hui and the open courtyard in front of it,

called the marae, are protected with an armour of tapu.

Made of soft wood, the whare hui is a big hall with a sloping roof and an entrance porch. Washed in red, the Polynesian colour of the sacred, the construction is symbolic of a highly esteemed ancestor. His image is placed on the peak of the sloping roof above the porch. Below it, on the front face of the peak, is the mask of a descendant. The beams of the façade sloping down from the mask are the primary ancestor's arms; they continue below the top of the side walls as fingers. His spine is the ridge-pole running horizontally along the apex, and the rafters angling down off it are the ribs. Therefore, when entering the whare hui, one walks into the body of the ancestor. The interior embellishments are visual summaries of Maori mythology and history. The poles holding up the 'spine' represent the connection between the Sky God and the Earth Goddess. Figures of the chief predecessors of other tribes are carved on the wall panels and those of the pioneering canoe captains on posts supporting the ridge-poles. Stories are also told through decorative wall panels displaying geometric designs fashioned from reeds and flax fibre.

The whare hui and the marae are the site of congregations and public ceremonies, which proceed in a clearly prescribed order and are preceded by the careful dismantling of tapu. To do this, the priest must invoke noa, the opposing, feminine force of tapu. On the meeting house, it is sometimes depicted on the lintel in the form of a female figure. A funeral and its associated welcome and farewell ceremonies are major events at meeting places. Death is an occasion for distant relatives and acquaintances from other villages to flock in support of the bereaved. Before the visitors can enter the marae, they must partake in the wero ('casting a spear') ritual – earlier conducted as proof of their peaceful intentions, but now maintained as a tradition and means to remove tapu. A warrior prances out of the marae and waves his spear in front of the calling party. He places an object on the ground, which must be picked up by a man from the visiting group.

Once the guests are allowed in, they are greeted with songs of welcome, speeches and hongi, the traditional nose-to-nose and forehead-to-forehead Maori greeting. The body lies in state in the building for three days, during which time there are more songs and reminiscences of the deceased. Commentaries are complimentary but can also have critical touches, and they are both solemn and humorous. The last night is one of fun and joking, the objective being to lighten the spirits of the bereaved family before they face the tough task of burying their loved one. After the burial in an adjacent cemetery, the mourners congregate in the whare and exchange thoughts on the past few days. Finally, it is time for the visitors to depart. They file out with a farewell hongi, and are sent off with song, and tapu once again closes over the mana of the marae and whare hui.

Mount Kailash & Lake Mansarovar
Tibet

At the heart of the world is an island called Jambudvipa, or the 'Continent of the Rose Apple Tree'. It is surrounded by oceans and other islands. It is the only place in the universe where human beings live, and from where they can attain enlightenment and transcend the entrapping cycle of life and death. From this island rises Mount Meru, the very centre of everything, temporal or spiritual. So hold ancient Hindu, Tantric Buddhist and Jain cosmological traditions. For followers of these faiths, the physical form of this mountain is Kailash, located deep within the remote and rugged high-altitude plateau of western Tibet. It is an inhospitable place, barren, windswept, thin of air, devoid of vegetation, almost bereft of shelter, and too cold to venture into for most part of the year. Days away from any substantial human habitation, Kailash is possibly the most difficult to access major sacred site in the world.

Though it peaks at only 6,700 metres above sea level – a relatively ordinary height in the Himalayas – Kailash is arresting because of its flat-sided, striated, snow-clad, pyramidal form. And because the mountains in its proximity are much lower, Kailash's striking form is all the more enhanced. Four great rivers of the Indian subcontinent spring forth from the region around the mountain. They are, from its east, south, west and

Facing page: A Tibetan family circles the awesome landscape dominated by Mt Kailash. Followers of the four religions that hold it sacred believe that the mountain should be respected and not scaled.

Prostrating at every step: only the toughest of pilgrims can adopt this punishing way to circle the holy mountain.

north, respectively, the mighty Tsang Po or Brahmaputra, the Karnali, the Sutlej, and the Indus.

Hindus believe Kailash to be the supreme abode of Shiva, the multi-faceted god. He lives on the summit with his wife Parvati, alternating austerities with gay abandon. Buddhists consider it the home of Chakrasamvara, a Tantric manifestation of the Buddha. According to legend, Buddhism prevailed over Bon, the pre-existing shamanist religion of Tibet, with the conquest of Kailash by Milarepa, the Indian sorcerer who is credited with reorganizing the decaying religion in the eleventh century. In a fierce battle, Milarepa bested the Bon master Naro Bonchung with a

last-minute flash of brilliant magic, arriving at the summit ahead of his amazed rival. Nevertheless, Bon practitioners continue to revere the peak as the dwelling place of Sipaimen, the sky goddess. For Jains, the mountain is Astapada, sacred due to its identification as the site where the soul of Rishabha or Adinatha, the first of their twenty-four tirthankaras (saints), attained liberation.

The lucky few who reach Kailash every year undertake the customary circumambulation of the peak. The extremely fit can manage the fifty-two kilometres in a single day, while those who choose the exacting method of prostrating and praying every step

of the way, can take up to three weeks. For the extremely devout and hardy, this is one half of the pilgrimage. For another, even longer trudge, awaits at Mansarovar, twenty-nine kilometres to the south. Kailash's associated holy lake shimmers an icy blue-green, challenging the devout to dip into its freezing waters in return for cleansing them of their sins. They may also walk its circumference, a round of 102 kilometres, touching five functioning monasteries enroute. It is a symbolic completion of the Wheel of Life.

Again, the option is to walk, or the optional mode of travel is by repeated prostrations. Myriad myths surround Mansarovar. The

lake (sarovar) was born in the mind (mana) of Brahma, the Creator. His sons prayed here, swans summer here, and in the wee hours of the morning, divine beings come here for the purest of baths. So did Queen Maya, the mother of Prince Siddhartha, later the Buddha. While in a dream-like state, she was whisked over by the gods for a ritual purification before conceiving her son.

To the west of Mansarovar is its antithesis, Rakshastal or Demon Lake. It is named after Ravana, the fearsome king of Lanka, from the Hindu epic *Ramayana*. Arrogant and cruel, Ravana was nevertheless a brilliant scholar, musician and warrior. He crossed the line, though,

Prayers printed on Buddhist flags are borne by the wind to the mountain.

The journey around the base of Mount Kailash, is spectacular but gruelling and is said to wipe out a whole lifetime of accrued sin.

when he decided to test his immense strength against the granite mass of Kailash. Shaken out of his meditation, the irascible Shiva showed him who was boss. With one toe, he pinned down the imperious maverick. A chastened Ravana had to sing Shiva's praises over thousands of years before the god released him. Rakshastal, where this happened, is beautiful like Mansarovar. However, the harshness of climate and terrain in its vicinity is unmitigated. For unlike at Mansarovar and Kailash, there is no Shiva, Buddha, Adinatha or Sipaimen here.

Mount Kenya
Kenya

The High God of the tribes that live on the flanks of Mt Kenya is the Ngai. There are various myths surrounding Ngai and his role in the origins of these people. The Kikuyu, who make up the majority of Kenya's populace, believe he created the first of their tribe, gave him a mate, and instructed them to set up home next to a fig tree on the highlands. This place, the Kikuyu Garden of Eden, is identified and considered sacred. It is entered through a blue gate, behind which are two mud huts, one for the first Kikuyu and the other for Mumbi, his wife. Ngai himself is supposed to be invisible and usually disinterested in the affairs of his people. He is not to be disturbed while all is well, and to that end, even regular prayers are discouraged. It is necessary to invoke him only at birth, initiation, marriage and death.

For the cattle-herding Maasai, Ngai was the owner of all the world's cattle. When heaven and earth separated, he bestowed the hoofed herds to the Maasai. Gift of the Great God, cattle are an integral part of Maasai rituals. Eating their meat and drinking their milk is believed to bring them closer to the deity. Ngai has both a benevolent and a vengeful aspect. His wife is Olapa, who once fought with and enraged her husband so much that he ripped out one of her eyes. That eye became the moon, and Olapa, thus, the Moon Goddess.

Ngai's home on earth is Mt Kenya. With a diameter of about a 100 kilometres, the mountain is actually a massif inclining over gentle, shallow slopes to climax in

Facing page: *Mt Kenya silhouetted against the dawn sky: an image that leaves few spiritually unmoved.*

Giant groundsel plants on the alpine heights of Mt. Kenya. There are eight different vegetation bands found on the mountain.

a bunch of several jagged peaks. More than two-and-a-half million years ago it was a live volcano. Because of the low viscosity of the lava that flowed, layer upon layer, the landform acquired a low profile resembling a shield (geologically termed 'shield volcano'). The craggy pinnacles are volcanic plugs, formations resulting from thick arms of lava solidifying within the vents, and left standing in isolation after the surrounding, softer hillsides eroded away.

Unlike the case of many other mountains considered sacred by local communities, climbing Mt Kenya is not taboo. Fifty years after it was first seen by the European missionary Johann Ludwig Krapf in 1849, the mountain's highest point, Batien, was finally scaled by the

pioneering geographer, Sir Harold Mackinder. Twentieth-century mountaineers, including the legendary Eric Shipton and Bill Tilman, followed to conquer the lower peaks. Despite lying close to the equator, where the sun shines fiercest, Mount Kenya carries snow on its higher reaches. As many as a dozen glaciers slide down its sides giving birth to numerous streams that water the Kenyan plains, including the country's largest river, the Tana.

From the hot savannah plains on the fringes, upto its highest point of 5,199 metres, Africa's second highest mountain supports astonishing biodiversity. The lowest levels, fertile with volcanic deposits, are heavily cultivated. Junipers and orchids higher up give way to a belt

Rising through thousands of feet, traversing a number of eco-zones, Mt Kenya is an agglomeration of interconnecting slopes, ridges and valleys.

of bamboo, followed by timberline forests. Still higher there are swathes of dense tangled brushwood and heaths. The needle-ice in the alpine zone restricts the vegetation to heather and tussock grass. Yet, scores of wildflowers bloom here almost the year round. Even in the rarefied atmosphere near the finials, sporadic greenery still lingers. Much of Africa's renowned wildlife roams Mt Kenya's sweeping slopes and valleys. They are the tramping grounds of the continent's big five; the elephant, buffalo, rhino, lion and leopard. Besides these, there are hyenas, hogs and handsome zebras, the graceful eland and other antelopes, and many species of monkeys and rodents. Birds of prey ride the thermals, while sunbirds, wagtails, ibis and hornbills forage in the forests.

A large part of the mountain block is a designated National Park. Yet all is not well. The glaciers are receding and human pressure on its resources continues. Scientists predict that in a few decades the snow and ice will vanish. The 'ostrich mountain' – as the Kikuyu call it, due to the ostrich-tail like appearance of the high tops, imparted by the speckled pattern of rock and snow – will have lost its plume. Traditionally, Ngai's tribal brood has oriented the doors of their homes to face the God's mountain home. Hopefully, he will not desert his worldly dwelling.

A Native American on his way to Ausangate, which has been a place of worship since ancient times.

Mount Ausangate & the Shrine of Qoyllur Rit'i

Peru

Native American tribes of the Andes have, since time immemorial, held certain mountains in the higher ranges, known as Apus, sacred. The reason for such belief was directly linked to the Indians's observation of how the mountain affected their life. They saw that the weather that came down to them in the form of rain, lightning or snow, first formed in the swirling mists around the peaks. The streams that gave them water began from glaciers slipping down its flanks. Good weather meant the right amount of water, and an abundant and timely harvest. Bad weather meant destruction by hail, flood or drought.

Towering almost 6,400 metres above sea level, Mt Ausangate is an Apu of the Vilcanota Andes. The Incas, when they rose to power in the fifteenth century, inducted it into their divine roll of honour. They worshipped the peak with gold. Legend has it that the death of Viracocha, father of King Pachacuti, who extended Inca dominions over most of South America, was foretold by comets emanating from Ausangate. The Quechua, largest of the region's Indian communities, believe that a palace, accessible only to the most accomplished shamans, exists within the depths of the mountain. Inside, the Apu's attendant cat

Lakes, glaciers and moraines riddle the terrain around Ausangate.

holds court. When the Spanish came to South America, they encouraged their own religion, Catholic Christianity, to make inroads into the existing faiths. In some cases, stories of Christian miracles emerged around sites already venerated by indigenous populations. One of these was in the remote Sinakara Valley, in the close vicinity of the Ausangate massif.

In 1780, it is related by the Church, a mestizo boy, Manuel, befriended Mariano, a young shepherd. Soon after, Mariano's herd prospered. As a reward, Mariano's father decided to buy both the boys new clothes. For this purpose, Manuel provided a sample cloth which turned out to be of the

same kind as worn by bishops. A local church party set off to investigate the curious case. On their approach, Manuel radiated a white light, and transformed into a tayakana shrub adorned with an image of the crucified Christ. Distressed at the thought of his friend coming to harm, Mariano fell dead and was buried under a rock. The rock was later painted with an image of Christ, and a crude church erected around it. The shrine became known as the Lord of Qoyllur Rit'i, Quechua for 'Star Snow'.

Several kilometres away from the nearest roadhead, Qoyllur Rit'i is a quiet place for most of the year. Around the time of the feasts of Ascension and Corpus Christi, it

becomes the focus of a large-scale pilgrimage, attracting up to 50,000 devotees across cultures and ethnic communities. Though the present ostensible 'pull' is of Our Señor of Star Snow, it is thought that, in its original form, the pilgrimage predates Qoyllur Rit'i, and was linked to reverence of Ausangate at the time of the year when the Pleiades constellation, an indicator of rain and harvest, was seen most clearly in the sky. Pilgrims trek up the dramatic landscape, organized in colourful groups or naciones from parishes in their villages. Led by the priest, the crew consists of dancers, musicians and lay people. Dressing styles vary across communities. Those from the Amazon lowlands wear feathered

headdresses, while the Aymara Indians sport knitted masks and hats. The signature personas of the pilgrimage are the ubiquitous Ukuku. Young men clad in shaggy coats and masks, they represent the mythical offspring of an Andean bear and woman. Ukuku play curious, seemingly contradictory, roles. On one hand they are the quintessential tricksters, free-wheeling through the processions, yelping, howling, creating disorder. Yet, they are also the pilgrimage policemen, ensuring conventions are adhered to, at times cracking their whips to good effect.

Inside the small shrine, fervent dancing continues unabated through the night. At daybreak, the Ukuku begin their climb

The annual pilgrimage to Quoyllur Rit'i attracts diverse groups, easily identifiable by the way they are dressed.

towards the snaking tongues of glaciers driving down from Ausangate. This inhospitable terrain is the haunt of the damned dead. Traditionally, the Ukuku must spend the night in the frozen landscape, battling and vanquishing these malevolent spirits, lighting giant candles and retrieving crosses left there a few days ago. Having proved their superhuman qualities, they descend the next morning carrying hunks of ice chipped out of the glaciers. Trapped inside the frozen essence of Ausangate is the light of the Star Snow. The melt will be ensconced in village chapels, from where it will radiate its holy energy for the next twelve months.

At the foot of Mt Ausangate – the snow-capped peaks of this area are the second largest Peruvian glaciated system.

Shrines of Difunta Correa & Gauchito Gil
Argentina

From the Bolivian border in the north to Tierra del Fuego in the extreme south, two sights recur on Argentinian roadsides. One is a small chapel-like structure, apparent more by the heaps of empty plastic bottles arranged around it than by its plain form. The other is more vivid due to its red-coloured boxy shape and ragged flags. They are both shrines of 'folk-saints', not accepted by the dominant Roman Catholic Church into its fold, yet often embellished with a cross. Both command wide following, especially amongst the common folk of the country who see in this no contradiction to their belief in Jesus. Although historically unproven, the legends of La Difunta Correa and Gauchito Gil, set more than 150 years ago, are too deeply ingrained to be swayed by the disapproval of the Christian clergy.

In the mid-nineteenth century, the nation of Argentina was in its birth throes. Civil wars ravaged the country. After the Spanish royalists were thrust aside, conflict continued between the Unitarios or Liberalists, who wanted the country to be united under a loose centralised rule, and the Federalists, who stood for regional autonomy. Recruited against his will by federalist forces, Baudillo, Maria Antonia Correa's husband, was whisked away to the war front. Hearing news of his having been taken ill and abandoned, Maria, carrying her infant son in her arms, set off on foot from her home in San Juan to look for him. It was to be a tragic trek, for thirst and hunger claimed

Facing page: *Plates of appreciation embedded inside the shrine of Gauchito Gil.*

One of several chapels at the main shrine of La Difunta Correa. Most of the articles at this one consist of framed pictures.

her in the harsh desert. When some passing muleteers came across her body, to their astonishment they found that though the mother's body lay lifeless, her suckling baby was alive, sustained, evidently, by milk flowing from her yet full breast. The story spread and the lady gained fame as La Difunta (the Defunct or Deceased) Correa, an icon of motherhood and miraculous acts.

Hailing from Mercedes, more than a thousand kilometres to the northeast, Antonio Mamerto Gil Nuñez was ensnared by the violent tumult of the same civil wars. He was a gaucho, or a cowboy, who paid the price of a romantic liaison with a widow by being chased by her brothers into the arms of the army. Antonio accredited himself

in battle and came back a hero, only to be shunted out again and thrown back into the war. This time he had had enough. He ran away, and lived as a fugitive 'Robin Hood', before being caught and beheaded. As he hung headfirst from the tree, awaiting the sword, he told his executioner that the latter's son was mortally ill and even though Gil was being killed, he would pray for the boy, who would be saved. After the bloody deed was done, the sergeant went home and discovered that what Gil had said was true. Filled with remorse and gratitude, he went back to the spot and erected a wooden cross. The disgraced deserter was now Gauchito Gil, saviour and worker of miracles.

Difunta Correa's main shrine is on a hill at Vallecito, near San Juan. What began as a modest little construction has now expanded into close to twenty different chapels, each dedicated to the type of prayer that has been made or answered. The assortment of offerings is amazingly diverse. There are wedding dresses from happy brides, and registration plates of old vehicles – even complete cars and motorcycles – replaced when new ones were acquired with La Difunta's grace. There are photographs of the sick in need of cure; academic certificates of successful students; sports paraphernalia like trophies, football jerseys and boxing gloves given by winners; kitchen appliances, statues and other miscellanea. In the main shrine, Difunta Correa's image lies

on a platform with her baby at her bosom. Outside, the shallow hillside is littered with model houses, grateful acknowledgements of homes that became reality with the saint's blessings.

The Gauchito's shrine is on the roadside near Mercedes. In the manner of a Latin American cowboy, he is depicted wearing a headband, chaps, belt, and rolled-up shirt sleeves. He is long-haired, mustachioed, and at times also bearded. The plethora of items placed at Gil's memorial is much the same as those at La Difunta Correa's. His colour is red, symbolic of innocent blood spilled, the colour of the Federalists, and the horse's blood he is supposed to have anointed himself with when

he became an outlaw. At his festival, held on the day he died, there is much singing, dancing and accordion playing, and a Ride of Faith saluting his occupation and life's events.

Travels of travail are integral to the legend of both saints, and for this reason, they are special to truck drivers who ply the lonely roads of Argentina's vast landscapes. In solemn remembrance of the intrepid mother's fatal thirst, they deposit empty bottles by the isolated shrines. The ritual at the good-hearted desperado's monument consists of tying a red pennant, or leaving behind an old automobile part. If nothing else, a toot of the horn suffices as a request for saintly protection on the highway.

Photographs and notes bearing messages from devotees cover the walls of a Difunta Correa shrine.

La Difunta lies lifelessly on the ground, with her baby at her breast, in a depiction of the legendary incident that led to the growth of her cult.

Palmyra

United States of America

Through the centuries, Christianity has experienced movements which have challenged prevalent spiritual practices and beliefs. These have often been characterised as Restorationist, because their aim has been to restore the church to what they considered to be its true nature. Often, they have led to the emergence of new communities with a unique set of beliefs. One such religious revival or 'awakening' occurred in North America in the first half of the nineteenth century, and led to the founding of what is popularly known as Mormonism. The little town of Palmyra, in western New York, was where its seminal events took place.

Joseph Smith, the man who started it all, lived on a farm on the outskirts of this settlement.

One day, in his early teens, a restless Smith went into the woods to pray. It was a time of great religious ferment in the region, and the young boy was unsure which denomination of Christianity he should drop his spiritual anchor in. His doubts were put to rest with what came to be known as the First Vision – a visit by God and his son Jesus. As related by him, the holy personages instructed him to refrain from embracing any of the existing churches, as they were all untrue. The surviving section of the forest where this happened is called the Sacred Grove. Today one can walk through the silent mass of trees on footpaths tagged with benches. Nearby, the log home and the more comfortable frame home, in which the Smith family lived, have been re-erected.

Later, Smith was to have several other divine visitations, which shaped the formulation of his religious ideas. The most momentous one directed him to Cumorah, a modest drumlin (hill formed by glacial activity), just over 100 feet high, on a neighbourhood farm. There, guided by the angel Moroni, Smith discovered a set of Golden Plates buried under a stone. On them was inscribed, in 'reformed Egyptian', the story of the Nephites on the continent, and the true lore of the church.

According to Mormon tradition, the prophet Lehi and his family migrated from Jerusalem to the coast of Arabia, approximately 600

Facing page: The Sacred Grove, where Joseph Smith received his First Vision.

Moroni's statue occupies the highest point on the Palmyra temple.

years before the birth of Christ. Lehi imparted long-held knowledge on the customs and history of Jews to his sons Laman and Nephi, and directed them to sail to America, the 'promised land'. There, the two brothers established independent nations named after them. Eventually, in the fourth century, the Lamanites destroyed the Nephites in a battle at Cumorah hill. Meanwhile, the history of the Nephites had been continuously recorded by a line of prophets in America, until Mormon, the last one, abridged the whole account, and inscribed it for posterity on gold plates. These, he bequeathed to his son, Moroni.

Between 1823 and 1830, Smith visited Cumorah several times, and translated the text of Moroni's unique inheritance, after which the angel took the Plates back. A few people close to Smith were allowed to see and handle the Plates. Martin Harris, a well-to-do farmer, was one of them. Finally, with the help the publisher Egbert Grandin, and financed partly by Harris, Smith's translations were published as the Book of Mormon. This is the main scripture of Mormonism. It is the Mormons' single most important differentiating identity from other branches of Christianity. Grandin's building, with its press machinery, bindery, and the shop which sold the first print-run of the Book of Mormon is preserved in Palmyra. A stone house now stands at the site of Harris' home.

Smith, and a small group of his associates, formally constituted the